Celtic Lent

The Bible Reading Fellowship
15 The Chambers, Vineyard
Abingdon OX14 3FE
brf.org.uk

The Bible Reading Fellowship (BRF) is a Registered Charity (233280)

ISBN 978 0 85746 637 2
First published 2018
Reprinted 2019 (twice)
10 9 8 7 6 5 4 3 2
All rights reserved

Acknowledgements
Unless otherwise acknowledged, scripture quotations are from The New Revised Standard Version of the Bible, Anglicised edition, copyright © 1989, 1995 by the Division of Christian Education of the National Council of the Churches of Christ in the United States of America. Used by permission. All rights reserved.

Scripture quotations taken from the Holy Bible, New Living Translation, copyright © 1996, 2004, 2007, 2013. Used by permission of Tyndale House Publishers, Inc., Carol Stream, Illinois 60188. All rights reserved.

Scripture quotations taken from The Holy Bible, New International Version (Anglicised edition) copyright © 1979, 1984, 2011 by Biblica. Used by permission of Hodder & Stoughton Publishers, a Hachette UK company. All rights reserved. 'NIV' is a registered trademark of Biblica. UK trademark number 1448790.

Scripture quotations taken from The Living Bible copyright © 1971 by Tyndale House Foundation. Used by permission of Tyndale House Publishers Inc., Carol Stream, Illinois 60188. All rights reserved.

p. 120: Lyrics from the song 'Broken Saviour' by Anam Caras Band. Used with permission. Copyright © Terry Braithwaite and Jackie Mills.

Every effort has been made to trace and contact copyright owners for material used in this resource. We apologise for any inadvertent omissions or errors, and would ask those concerned to contact us so that full acknowledgement can be made in the future.

A catalogue record for this book is available from the British Library

Printed and bound by CPI Group (UK) Ltd, Croydon CR0 4YY

Celtic Lent

40 days of devotions to Easter

David Cole

Contents

Introduction

Lent is a significant part of the Christian calendar. It is a period where we endeavour to lessen our intake by fasting and giving things up, and to increase our focus on things divine, with particular attention paid to the coming crucifixion and resurrection of Jesus Christ. For the Celtic Christians, this was a deeply significant part of their year, a time which they took seriously with their fasting and focus.

What is commonly referred to today as Celtic Christianity is the expression of the Christian faith from the Irish and British churches, and those kingdoms throughout what is now England and Scotland. These churches were influenced by this style and expression of the Christian faith rather than the expression of the Christian faith that was more prominent in the Latin church growing out of the Roman Empire. Much of the kingdoms of the Angles and, to some extent, the Saxon kingdoms were heavily influenced by Celtic Christianity.

Although there was only one 'church', there were distinct differences at that time between the practices of this Celtic tradition and the Latin, or Roman, church (not to be mistaken with the modern Roman Catholic church) in certain theologies and ways of expressing the Christian faith. This enables us to suggest that there was a 'Celtic Christianity'. Despite the distinct differences within the Celtic churches themselves, there were enough similarities within the cultures and people, and so therefore the churches as well, for us to be able to say that Celtic Christianity certainly was a distinct expression of the Christian faith found in Britain, Ireland and some of northern Europe.[1]

In this book, designed to take you through Lent with daily devotionals from Ash Wednesday to Easter Sunday, we will encounter some of that distinct expression and some of the teachings and theology found in the works, writings and monastic Rules of the Celtic saints. We will also discover some of the more modern expressions and inspirations of Celtic Christianity that flow within current streams of Christianity.

For the largest section of our journey towards Easter, we will weave together days of discovery and adventure in Celtic Christianity with excerpts from Celtic saints' teaching relevant to Lent, as well as stories of their lives, ancient and modern. The Celtic saints wrote numerous Rules and apostolic-style letters, as well as greater pieces which we will be dipping into. We will also look at different aspects of Celtic theology relevant to Lent. This will include aspects of eucharistic liturgies we have, such as the Stowe Missal; the theology of the whole of creation being reconciled back to God through the work of the cross (as found in Romans 8, for example), which was deeply engrained in Celtic Christianity; and modern teachings and writings on Celtic Christianity. For Holy Week itself, however, we will be illuminating specifically the story of *The Dream of the Rood*, a seventh/eighth-century Celtic/Anglo-Saxon saga of the cross of Christ.

There will also be a chance each Sunday to reflect and contemplate something specific to allow God to reveal even more deeply the things we are unfolding.

As you use this book to help guide you towards resurrection in this season of Lent, I pray that God will challenge and encourage you, build up and dismantle things within your heart, soul and spirit, so that through the inspiration of an ancient aspect of our spiritual heritage, you will become closer to God and grow more and more in the divine character as you allow yourself to be transformed.

Ash Wednesday
to Sunday

Ash Wednesday

This is a day to remember the reason that Christ had to come to die on the cross. Lent begins with a direct focus on the end – the crucifixion – and the need for our reconciliation with God because of sin in life. Ash Wednesday focuses on the punishment God gave to Adam and Eve in the Judaic/Christian creation story, and the statement from Genesis 3:19 that we, as humans, came from dust (or ashes) and will return to the same.

In an ancient Irish story of the creation of Adam, which survived as part of 'imaginative reworkings and complementary additions to the canon'[2] of scripture, Adam is made not just from the dust of the earth, but from seven different components: earth, sea, sun, clouds, wind, stones and the light of the world. These correspond, in the same order, to: his body, blood, countenance, thoughts, breath, bones and soul (also connected to the Holy Spirit, or the divine image within us). These, in turn, relate to personality traits within human beings.

> If in someone the part that is the earth is dominant, then that person will be indolent. If it be the sun, they will be attractive and vivacious. If it be clouds, they will be irresponsible and lustful. If the wind dominates, they will be fiery and irascible. If it be the stones, they will be severe, both thieving and grasping. If it be the sea, they will be likable and placid, and will be beautiful. If it is the light that is the strongest, they will know their own mind, and will be filled with the grace of the Holy Spirit and divine scripture.[3]

This imaginative expression of different aspects of creation being a part of who we each are, and that we will possibly have one which is more dominant, is typical of the beautiful creative mind of the Celtic Christians. This particular imaginative expression gives us an even closer connection to the whole of creation. It isn't just the dust or earth that we are created from, but different elements found in the whole of creation, each interwoven within us, plus the inclusion of the Holy Spirit, that is, the divine image within our being. This gives us a much deeper, more interconnected relationship with creation – another very Celtic understanding. All of this, of course, was marred by the incoming of sin into the beautifully, perfectly created cosmos which God had formed with love, which humanity was a part of.

So we begin Lent by reminding ourselves that we were created from part (or parts) of the physical creation, and that our bodies will return to the creation at their end.

Contemplation

Close your eyes and visualise the creation of Adam. But imagine it as described in the Irish retelling of the story, from those seven different aspects of the natural world: not only the dust of the ground, but earth, sea, sun, clouds, wind, stones and the light of the world as the divine image placed within us. How might this description, if these seven components are metaphorically a part of us, help us feel more connected to the natural world which surrounds us? How much more might we mourn for the coming of sin into creation which separates all things from its Creator?

Reading

[Adam and Eve] hid from the Lord God among the trees. Then the Lord God called to the man, 'Where are you?'

He replied, 'I heard you walking in the garden, so I hid. I was afraid because I was naked.'

'Who told you that you were naked?' the Lord God asked.

'Have you eaten from the tree whose fruit I commanded you not to eat?'

The man replied, 'It was the woman you gave me who gave me the fruit, and I ate it.'

Then the Lord God asked the woman, 'What have you done?'

'The serpent deceived me,' she replied. 'That's why I ate it.'

Then the Lord God said to the serpent, 'Because you have done this, you are cursed more than all animals, domestic and wild. You will crawl on your belly, grovelling in the dust as long as you live. And I will cause hostility between you and the woman, and between your offspring and her offspring. He will strike your head, and you will strike his heel.'

Then he said to the woman, 'I will sharpen the pain of your pregnancy, and in pain you will give birth. And you will desire to control your husband, but he will rule over you.'

And to the man he said, 'Since you listened to your wife and ate from the tree whose fruit I commanded you not to eat, the ground is cursed because of you. All your life you will struggle to scratch a living from it. It will grow thorns and thistles for you, though you will eat of its grains. By the sweat of your brow will you have food to eat until you return to the ground from which you were made. For you were made from dust, and to dust you will return.'

GENESIS 3:8–19 (NLT)

Prayer

Great Creator of life, the universe and everything, who fashioned humanity from the created world, I repent of the sin in my life, both those things known to me and unknown. I repent of any actions which have harmed the world from which I am made. I ask your forgiveness, and am reminded, by the ash of this day, that my body will one day cease to function. But I praise you also that, because of your grace and mercy, the essence of who I am shall continue forever. Amen

Thursday

The purpose of giving something up for Lent is so that when we reach the Easter weekend and focus on the cross of Christ, we have a small idea of what it is to make a sacrifice. But do we really understand what it means to sacrifice something of ourselves for God?

In the *Cambrai Homily*,[4] a sixth/seventh-century Irish writing, when looking at the passage in Matthew's gospel which speaks of taking up our cross (Matthew 16:24), it says, 'To take our cross upon ourselves means to accept loss and martyrdom and to suffer for Christ's sake.'[5] It then goes on to describe three different types of martyrdom – white, green (or blue[6]) and red martyrdom.

White martyrdom is when one gives up everything they love, be that comforts of home, title or position: that is, giving up one's known life(style). This was to 'die' to your old life and be committed to the life God draws you to. This is what many of the Celtic saints did in giving up their social positions, be it in a royal household, such as Melangell and Hilda, or a position of nobility or in the military, such as Cuthbert and Illtyd, to become monks and nuns.

Green martyrdom was when one committed to spiritual disciplines or exercises, such as fasting or prayer vigils: to give up some form of comfort or nicety to be committed to a spiritual discipline. This could be for a selected period or for life. So, in essence, each of us who gives up something for Lent is practising this ancient Celtic idea of green martyrdom, for a short time at least.

Red martyrdom was giving one's physical life up to death for the sake of Christ and one's faith: the traditional understanding of martyrdom.

'These three kinds of martyrdom,' the *Cambrai Homily* says, 'take place in those people who repent well, who control their desires, or who shed their blood… for Christ's sake.'[7]

The question is, how far are we willing to go for the sake of our faith? Green martyrdom for Lent is one thing, but what about committing to spiritual exercises for a longer period of time, or even for life? How many of us would be willing to give up everything we know as our current life and take up a new life, perhaps not quite so privileged, for the sake of a call from God – like so many missionaries have done over the centuries, and still do? And finally, when we read that we are to take up our cross – that is, to give up ourselves to Christ – are we willing to risk the possibility of actually giving up our lives as many saints have done throughout history?

We may have given something up for Lent, but what about beyond that?

Contemplation

Think about what you have given up in the past for the sake of God, perhaps even just what you have given up this Lent. How much of a sacrifice has it been, really? Look again at the descriptions of white, green and red martyrdom. Contemplate what you might be willing to give up for God from now on, beyond Lent.

Reading

From then on Jesus began to tell his disciples plainly that it was necessary for him to go to Jerusalem, and that he would suffer many terrible things at the hands of the elders, the leading priests, and the teachers of religious law. He would be killed, but on the third day he would be raised from the dead.

But Peter took him aside and began to reprimand him for saying such things. 'Heaven forbid, Lord,' he said. 'This will never happen to you!'

Jesus turned to Peter and said, 'Get away from me, Satan! You are a dangerous trap to me. You are seeing things merely from a human point of view, not from God's.'

Then Jesus said to his disciples, 'If any of you wants to be my follower, you must give up your own way, take up your cross, and follow me. If you try to hang on to your life, you will lose it. But if you give up your life for my sake, you will save it. And what do you benefit if you gain the whole world but lose your own soul? Is anything worth more than your soul? For the Son of Man will come with his angels in the glory of his Father and will judge all people according to their deeds.

MATTHEW 16:21–27 (NLT)

Prayer

Lord Jesus Christ, as I contemplate over this Lent period the sacrifice you made at the cross, give me the strength of heart to be willing to give up whatever you desire of me, be that simple things for a short time, the whole of my life as I know it, or even my life itself, knowing that you are with me always. Amen

Friday

Many people are dedicated to physical fitness and exercise. I have friends who go out on 'Park Runs' each week, and a number who regularly run marathons for charity. These things don't just happen; they have to be trained for. There has to be some form of fitness regime and focused dedication to be able to stay fit. Some people are very determined to have the fittest body, and so are more dedicated at keeping up with the regime. Other people are happy to have a body which just stays at the level of fitness which is comfortable for them, so they train a little, but not too much. Still others aren't that bothered at all. The level of physical fitness which you want to achieve and maintain will determine the amount of effort you put in to make it and sustain it, and the amount of effort you put in to your physical fitness will have a direct result on how fit your body gets and stays.

Just as this is the case for our physical selves, so it is the case for our inner and spiritual selves.

Yesterday, we looked at an ancient text which spoke of green martyrdom. Today, we will dip into a modern book on Celtic Christianity which has a chapter on green martyrdom and spiritual fitness.

In *Water from an Ancient Well*, Kenneth McIntosh begins this chapter with a story of a man going into a gym to look around to see whether he wants to join, only to find that no one is working out; they are simply sitting around. In the weights room, people are reading weight-lifting magazines; the same scenario by the running machines with relevant magazines – all throughout the gym. Frustrated by what he sees, the man speaks to the woman showing him around at the end and says:

> 'What on earth is wrong with these people?… No one is working out… What kind of crazy place is this?' 'Oh,' the woman sniffs, 'You must be looking for one of those old-fashioned health clubs where… they make people feel guilty if they don't get on the machines… Our members all agree that they are happier not exerting themselves – life's hard enough without making our muscles do all that unpleasant exercise.'[8]

McIntosh is, of course, using this ridiculous story (which is much funnier in full as he tells it) to parallel the spiritual life without spiritual disciplines, and he says, 'Contemporary Christianity is often a lot like a non-exercising health club.'[9] In the same chapter, he goes on to say this:

> The ancient Celts… engaged in robust spiritual exercises; they weren't afraid of 'sweat'. The stories of Anthony of Egypt inspired them… They paid attention when Anthony spoke of *ascesis*, a Greek word that literally translates 'rigor' and denotes spiritual discipline. Furthermore – and this had great impact on Celtic spirituality – Anthony insisted that *ascesis* required physical practices.[10]

The Celtic Christians took green martyrdom seriously, partly because this could include the lay people who had everyday jobs, such as the farmers, etc. who were connected with the monastic community; it wasn't just for the monks and nuns who had committed to white martyrdom as well. We too can commit to this green martyrdom, this idea of practising spiritual disciplines.

Contemplation

Leading on from yesterday's contemplation, spend time with God now, as if God was showing you around a spiritual gym. What disciplines are you willing to commit to in order to bring up the fitness level of your inner and spiritual self? Remember, the amount of effort put in will directly affect the level of fitness – for example, if you build up to practising an hour of silent contemplative prayer each day, you will have a much greater sense of divine peace than someone who does just a minute of it, or none at all.

Reading

Do you not know that in a race the runners all compete, but only one receives the prize? Run in such a way that you may win it. Athletes exercise self-control in all things; they do it to receive a perishable garland, but we an imperishable one. So I do not run aimlessly, nor do I box as though beating the air; but I punish my body and enslave it, so that after proclaiming to others I myself should not be disqualified.

1 CORINTHIANS 9:24–27

Prayer

Gracious, loving one, you have given me a body to care for, but it is not separate from my soul and spirit. May I see that each are as important as the other. May I be committed to the spiritual disciplines which you draw me to so that I can be as spiritually fit as I can be. Amen

Saturday

After the legalisation of Christianity by the Emperor Constantine in the early fourth century, the church in the Roman Empire quickly became interwoven with the political empire. For some, the depth of spirituality lessened as, 'since the bishop now functioned as a political figure, many of his religious decisions favoured the empire rather than the church'.[11] Many of those who wanted to stay true to their faith, rather than sit in this new collusion with the empire, fled the urbanisation and sought sanctuary in the deserts. They fled both in solitude and in groups of cenobitic (community-based) 'monks' – the latter practising being alone together. This is seen by many as the birth of monasticism.

'These individuals usually renounced their material possessions and practised a deep degree of self-sacrifice that recalled the spirit of Christians facing persecution in the earliest Christian communities.'[12] Contrary to the growing urbanised church of the empire, who were spending a great deal of this time creating 'orthodox' theology and creeds and vying for position, the Desert Fathers and Mothers 'neither courted the approval of their contemporaries nor sought to provoke their disapproval, because [even] the opinions of others had ceased, for them, to be matters of importance'.[13]

This ascetic Christianity of the Desert Fathers and Mothers inspired the tribal/community-based Christians of Britain and Ireland. The influence of Desert monasticism was greater on the formation of Celtic monasticism and on the development of their way of life than the parochial church-based Christianity growing from the empire. It is said that Martin of Tours went to the deserts and brought this monastic way back to Tours (interestingly, an urban setting), and some of the early Celtic saints, such as Ninian, are said to have gone to Tours and were inspired to bring this monastic expression back to Britain and Ireland. Cassian (fourth century) was also a great influence on the Celtic monasticism, with his teachings of the desert monastics. The only trouble was that there were not really any deserts in these Celtic lands. But the fact that there are still place names in Wales and Ireland which translate as 'desert' shows that they found a way of appropriating this monastic way into the land in which they lived.

The Desert Fathers and Mothers inspired the Celtic saints to what they later called green and white martyrdom – the giving up of life and possessions to become wholly dedicated to God and the spiritual path. Monasticism was the foundation of the Celtic model of Christian community; the concepts of green and white martyrdom were widely spread; and spiritual disciplines were at the core of the practical outworking of their faith. Over the next week, we will take a look at the lives of some of the Celtic Christians who did just this: gave up the lives they had to live a life dedicated to God.

Contemplation

Martin of Tours and Cassian brought Desert monasticism in to their own settings and appropriated it for where they were. The Celtic saints took it to Britain and Ireland and appropriated it for *their* own setting. How might you be able to appropriate it for your own setting?

Reading

You then, my child, be strong in the grace that is in Christ Jesus; and what you have heard from me through many witnesses entrust to faithful people who will be able to teach others as well. Share in suffering like a good soldier of Christ Jesus. No one serving in the army gets entangled in everyday affairs; the soldier's aim is to please the enlisting officer. And in the case of an athlete, no one is crowned without competing according to the rules. It is the farmer who does the work who ought to have the first share of the crops. Think over what I say, for the Lord will give you understanding in all things.

2 TIMOTHY 2:1–7

Prayer

God of all ages and places, God of all peoples and cultures, help me to be able to take the riches from the spiritual heritage that I have and appropriate them into my own context, so that I can be closer to you through ancient tried practices. Amen

Contemplation
for the first **Sunday** in Lent

The Celtic Christians practised green martyrdom,
the dedication to spiritual disciplines.
How might you do this more in your life?

Week one

Monday

Hilda was a princess of the East Angles. The kingdom was of the same family line as the Northumbrian kingdom, and so had very close connections.

For a little over 30 years, Hilda lived as a princess in the royal courts in East Anglia. The likelihood is that she would have been married by that time and probably had children. Nothing is ever mentioned of either a husband or children by Bede or any other historian, but unless there was a specific reason which prevented it, a princess then would certainly be married by the age of 30. Perhaps her husband died in battle, or of some disease. Perhaps her children too, or perhaps she was unable to have children of her own. Whatever the particular circumstances, for the first 30 years of her life Hilda lived the royal life as a princess in a powerful royal family, protected by the palace walls and royal guards.

Hilda had encountered a bishop, Paulinus, of the Roman church when she was in her teens, and had been baptised along with her relative King Edwin of Northumbria. Life seemed to be set for Hilda, but a few years later things changed.

King Edwin was killed in battle, and the Northumbrian people had reverted to paganism in subjection to the conquering king, Penda of Mercia. However, Edwin's successor, Oswald, came to the Northumbrian throne and drove Penda back across the Northumbrian borders into Mercia. Having been raised on or near Iona in safety from the waring kingdoms, he was brought up in the Irish/Celtic expression of the Christian faith, which differed slightly from the Latin/Roman expression of the faith. He wanted to have a Christian mission across his new kingdom, and so invited monks from Iona to come. The first mission failed, but the second mission, led by Bishop Aidan, was vastly successful.

Hilda, who had lived for at least a decade in the Roman style of Christianity as a princess, encountered this mission at some point and was so taken by it that an *anam chara* (Soul Friend) friendship grew between her and Aidan. She saw in Aidan something more than she had ever seen in other bishops, something which reflected Christ more authentically, perhaps. This 'Celtic' way of living the Christian faith obviously resonated with her spirit, as she began to live it out herself from then on.

In her early 30s, Hilda decided that simply living out this faith as a princess wasn't enough; she wanted to be a nun. So she made the choice of both green and white martyrdom and left the royal palace to travel to France where a relative of hers was already a nun. Bishop Aidan heard of her leaving and sent a message that he wished her to stay, as Britain needed her. He gave her a plot of land on which she could build her own monastic centre. Later, she ran a centre in Hartlepool, which was a joint monastic centre with the first, and finally Hilda ran the large double monastic centre (that is, having both monks and nuns as well as lay people and a large community) in Whitby, which hosted arguably the most significant meeting in Celtic/Roman church history: the Synod of Whitby in 664.

Hilda had lived a life of privilege and of standing. She was a royal princess in one of the most powerful families in Britain. But something within her was stirred and she felt called by God to give it all up and take on a monastic habit instead.

Contemplation

Hilda not only gave up her lifestyle as a princess, but she also gave up the way she had been living the Christian faith for one which she saw as more authentic. These were two huge aspects of her life to lay aside. What are you willing to lay aside to become closer to God? Are you willing to lay aside the way you currently live the Christian life if you felt another way resonated with you more?

Reading

Then she started to return with her daughters-in-law from the country of Moab, for she had heard in the country of Moab that the Lord had considered his people and given them food. So she set out from the place where she had been living, she and her two daughters-in-law, and they went on their way to go back to the land of Judah. But Naomi said to her two daughters-in-law, 'Go back each of you to your mother's house. May the Lord deal kindly with you, as you have dealt with the dead and with me. The Lord grant that you may find security, each of you in the house of your husband.' Then she kissed them, and they wept aloud. They said to her, 'No, we will return with you to your people.' But Naomi said, 'Turn back, my daughters, why will you go with me? Do I still have sons in my womb that they may become your husbands? Turn back, my daughters, go your way, for I am too old to have a husband. Even if I thought there was hope for me, even if I should have a husband tonight and bear sons, would you then wait until they were grown? Would you then refrain from marrying? No, my daughters, it has been far more bitter for me than for you, because the hand of the Lord has turned against me.' Then they wept aloud again. Orpah kissed her mother-in-law, but Ruth clung to her.

So she said, 'See, your sister-in-law has gone back to her people and to her gods; return after your sister-in-law.' But Ruth said, 'Do not press me to leave you or to turn back from following you! Where you go, I will go; where you lodge, I will lodge; your people shall be my people, and your God my God. Where you die, I will die – there will I be buried. May the Lord do thus and so to me, and more as well, if even death parts me from you!'

When Naomi saw that she was determined to go with her, she said no more to her.

So the two of them went on until they came to Bethlehem.

RUTH 1:6–19

Prayer

Thank you, Lord, that you change who we are throughout our lives, and that you draw us closer to you. May I be willing to give up whatever you ask me to for your sake. Amen

Tuesday

Illtyd was a commander of soldiers. We first meet him in his life story as he is catching up with his soldiers as they travel across the Welsh hillsides.

As a commander of soldiers, Illtyd would most likely have come from a family of good standing and stepped into his role as an expectation. As far as we know, he didn't have any issue with that expectation. Despite being of military standing, however, and commanding soldiers in a time when war was rife, it seems that Illtyd was a man who had a good heart and had compassion.

Illtyd's soldiers had gone ahead of him across the hillside and had come across a hermit. When Illtyd arrived, his soldiers were harassing the hermit, treating him badly and disrespecting the hermit's dwelling and meagre belongings.

Illtyd, ashamed of his soldiers' behaviour, chastised them and sent them off. Illtyd got off his horse and went to speak to the hermit, who, he discovered, was called Cadoc. Illtyd was so taken by the fact that Cadoc would not and did not retaliate to the behaviour of the soldiers that he wanted to know more about why this was. Cadoc spoke to Illtyd about the spiritual battle between the powers of light and darkness, about the power of the cross of Christ and that he was a soldier, just like Illtyd, but in a very different way. This was why he had not reacted to the soldiers' treatment of him, because of the words and instructions of Cadoc's 'commander', Jesus Christ.

Illtyd went home with these words ringing in his ears and resting heavily upon his heart. That night, in a dream, God spoke to Illtyd and told him that he was called to put down the armour and weapons of the world and to take up arms in the spiritual battle instead. As soon as Illtyd awoke, he did exactly that, leaving his privileged military life behind him and going to Cadoc to train in the spiritual battle.

Illtyd stayed with Cadoc as a hermit, in the practice of both green and white martyrdom, until he founded his own monastic centre.

Illtyd then trained many other people, including David, now patron saint of Wales, and Gildas the Wise, first chronicler of the English/ British church in 'On the Ruin of Britain'.

Contemplation

How do you understand the spiritual battle? With what do you 'fight'? Do you try to apply the world's way of doing things to the spiritual conflict? Do you put on the world's armour? Or do you fight with divine weaponry?

Reading

Indeed, we live as human beings, but we do not wage war according to human standards; for the weapons of our warfare are not merely human, but they have divine power to destroy strongholds. We destroy arguments and every proud obstacle raised up against the knowledge of God, and we take every thought captive to obey Christ. We are ready to punish every disobedience when your obedience is complete.

Look at what is before your eyes. If you are confident that you belong to Christ, remind yourself of this, that just as you belong to Christ, so also do we.

2 CORINTHIANS 10:3–7

Prayer

Thank you, defender God, that you give us what we need to fight against the spiritual darkness, to be able to stand for you and to destroy strongholds. May all that is in me that is not of you fall subject to these things. Amen

Wednesday

Cuthbert was most likely of noble birth in a family of the Northumbrian Angles. Although we know nothing of his parentage, there are allusions in his life story to his social standing. One is that he was given to the care of a woman named Kenswith when he was young to be brought up; another is that he was able to have the time to excel in sport and gymnastics; and finally that he had a horse and servant. It seems that from childhood, Cuthbert was brought up in the Christian faith. He grew up in Northumbria at the time of Aidan's missions, so it is chronologically possible that as a young boy Cuthbert heard Aidan himself speak. Whether he did or not, we can be sure that Cuthbert would have been taught the Celtic Christian faith of the monastic centre on Lindisfarne. It is almost certain, because of Cuthbert's family, that he would have entered the military at a fairly young age, around his early to mid-teens. In some tourist information literature in Dunbar, it is suggested that Cuthbert may have been at the military base there, which is where the ruins of Dunbar castle now stand.

One night, as Cuthbert sat out on the hill with some shepherds (perhaps the sheep belonging to the military base), he saw the soul of Bishop Aidan being lifted to heaven at the moment of Aidan's death. Upon seeing this vision, Cuthbert's heart was stirred. He decided then and there that he would step into the green and white martyrdom the Celtic saints spoke of and leave his life and family, and whatever future that may have meant, and become a monk. Despite the fact that he was close to Lindisfarne, Cuthbert chose to go to the monastic centre at Melrose on the Northumbrian mainland.

He arrived at the front door of the monastery carrying a spear (perhaps for protection on the journey), on a horse, with a servant walking next to him. When he got to the monastery, he got off his horse, gave his spear and cloak to his servant, handed him the reins of the horse, and walked into the monastery with nothing but the clothes he wore.

This act at the monastery door was a great symbolic act of him totally giving up his old life in complete dedication to Christ, and stepping into the new life of a monk.

Contemplation

As we journey along life's path, what things do we hold dear to us? What aspects of our upbringing and social standing mean a lot to us? Are you willing to give these things up for the sake of God if you felt God ask you to? Think about what you have that you might struggle to give up if God asked you to go somewhere with nothing.

Reading

Then someone came to [Jesus] and said, 'Teacher, what good deed must I do to have eternal life?' And he said to him, 'Why do you ask me about what is good? There is only one who is good. If you wish to enter into life, keep the commandments.' He said to him, 'Which ones?' And Jesus said, 'You shall not murder; You shall not commit adultery; You shall not steal; You shall not bear false witness; Honour your father and mother; also, You shall love your neighbour as yourself.' The young man said to him, 'I have kept all these; what do I still lack?' Jesus said to him, 'If you wish to be perfect, go, sell your possessions, and give the money to the poor, and you will have treasure in heaven; then come, follow me.' When the young man heard this word, he went away grieving, for he had many possessions.

MATTHEW 19:16–22

Prayer

Gracious Lord, thank you for all the provision you have gifted me. Thank you for the privilege of all that living where I live offers me. May I hold these things lightly compared to the strength by which I hold on to you and your calling upon me. Make me willing to give up whatever I have to follow you, if you so desired. Amen

Thursday

Columba had been on mission around his native Ireland for some time before he entered a monastic centre to be trained as a monk. He was of noble birth of the family of the High Kings of Ireland; it was part of the life of the High Kings to be 'married' to the land, so a deep love of his homeland would have been in Columba's blood.

When Columba entered the monastic life for formal training, he went to the centre of Finnian at Clonard. As part of his life and meditations at the monastery, as many of the monks did, he copied out scripture in the Scriptorium. When it came time for him to leave after his training had finished, Columba wanted to take the 'Cathach', the book of Psalms which he had created, with him and place it in his own monastery somewhere in his beloved Ireland. However, Finnian was not going to let the book go. You see, not only had Columba copied out the book of Psalms, but he had also copied out the personal margin notes, or introductory notes to each chapter, the interpretive rubric before each psalm which Finnian had added when he had written the book which Columba had copied.[14] Finnian felt that the notes were far too personal to leave the monastic centre he was in.

Columba became greatly upset about this as he had spent time, although it is thought perhaps 'at night in haste by a miraculous light', copying out the book. Finnian, however, would not back down. Columba took his complaint to the authorities and a legal decision was to be made by King Diarmait Mac Cerbhaill. Both Finnian and Columba gave their sides of the story, and the decision was made that 'to every cow her calf, to every book its copy'. Therefore, Columba had to leave the copy he had made with the original in Clonard.

It isn't entirely clear exactly what happened to lead to what followed. Perhaps it was a rumour which made the High King feel that a member of his bloodline was being mistreated and so he needed to stand up for him; perhaps it was something else entirely. Whatever it was, following this decision, a battle flared up: the battle of Cul Dremhne, in which many soldiers were killed, and the Cathach passed into the hands of the O'Donnells. Distraught, Columba pledged to make amends. However, either he was banished from Ireland for the enormity of the bloodshed, or he decided that he would give up his beloved Ireland on the advice of his Soul Friend, Malaise. Either way, Columba ended up leaving Ireland and founding his monastic centre on Iona instead.

Columba gave up his life twice, as it were: once giving up his life of the family of the High Kings, and then again he gave up his life in Ireland, never to return, to go and minister to the Picts in what we now know as northern Scotland.

Once again, the green and white martyrdom of the Celtic saints was embodied in the life of one of its greatest names.

Contemplation

Sometimes we do things which cause us to have to give things up. We may find ourselves in a place where we have to let go of things; we don't want to, but we have to because it is the consequence of our actions. When you find yourself in these situations, or if you can imagine yourself being in such a situation, how willing are you to lose the things which you love, or give them up, because you have to?

Reading

In the morning David wrote a letter to Joab, and sent it by the hand of Uriah. In the letter he wrote, 'Set Uriah in the forefront of the hardest fighting, and then draw back from him, so that he may be struck down and die.' As Joab was besieging the city, he assigned Uriah to the place where he knew there were valiant warriors. The men of the city came out and fought with Joab; and some of the servants of David among the people fell. Uriah the Hittite was killed as well. Then Joab sent and told David all the news about the fighting…

When the wife of Uriah heard that her husband was dead, she made lamentation for him. When the mourning was over, David sent and brought her to his house, and she became his wife, and bore him a son. But the thing that David had done displeased the Lord, and the Lord sent Nathan to David…

David said to Nathan, 'I have sinned against the Lord.' Nathan said to David, 'Now the Lord has put away your sin; you shall not die. Nevertheless, because by this deed you have utterly scorned the Lord, the child that is born to you shall die.' Then Nathan went to his house.

2 SAMUEL 11:14–18; 11:26—12:1; 12:13–15

Prayer

Gracious, loving God, sometimes we do things which are against your will. Sometimes we do things unintentionally which cause bad results. Thank you that, even in those times, even if there are consequences of our actions, we can rely upon your grace in our repentance and discover a new path ahead. Amen

Friday

Brendan the navigator was born in the Munster region of Ireland and was trained in the monastic way from birth by both Erc and Ita. At around age six or seven, he went to the monastic school of Tuam and was taught by Iarlaithe mac Loga, before moving to Clonard as a young adult learning under Finnian, where he was one of the twelve apostles of Ireland who trained there. Brendan's father was Findlug, a descendant of Alta of the line of Eógan, possibly Eógan mac Néill, also known as the first king of Tyrone, and the son of Niall of the Nine Hostages.

Brendan was known as an ascetical man and as an adult became the spiritual 'father' to almost 3,000 monks. Suffice to say, Brendan had good lineage and a good reputation as a leading monk. However, he was willing to give this all up when presented with a chance of a great sea adventure. This adventure, known as Brendan's Voyage,[15] could well have cost Brendan his life. Setting out into the unknown western sea, he could, as far as he knew, be setting sail to the edge of the world where he would sail either right off the edge or right into paradise; either way, he might never be coming back. He was willing to give up everything he knew to follow this dream sparked by the stories of a monk named Barinthus.

After a period of prayer, Brendan and 14 other monks set sail into the unknown. They encountered great adventure and danger, tremendous toil and miracles; they spent times wondering whether they would ever make it back alive. All of them were willing to step into white martyrdom which could easily lead to red martyrdom – but why? Because they believed that this was what God had called them to be doing at this time. They stepped out in faith despite what dangers there might have been because they wholeheartedly believed in living out the scripture which says that the one born of the Spirit is like the wind, blown from somewhere to who knows where else (John 3:8). They were fully open to moving wherever God took them.

This was at the heart of the Celtic saints' understanding of green and white martyrdom: the total openness to the move of the divine Spirit and the drive of God to take them and send them wherever God wanted to send them, to go where they were sent, or even drift where they were taken, for some who set out to sea.

Brendan and his monks gave up all they knew to follow the divine call and discover new things.

Contemplation

Sometimes we may feel the desire or call to do something which seems impossible. Having spent time with God, Brendan believed that this adventurous voyage was what God had called him to do. How willing are you to set out into an unknown? Whether that be physically like Brendan, or inwardly, or even within work or relationships. With divine guidance, how willing are you to launch into something unknown?

Reading

On that day, when evening had come, he said to them, 'Let us go across to the other side.' And leaving the crowd behind, they took him with them in the boat, just as he was. Other boats were with him. A great gale arose, and the waves beat into the boat, so that the boat was already being swamped. But he was in the stern, asleep on the cushion; and they woke him up and said to him, 'Teacher, do you not care that we are perishing?' He woke up and rebuked the wind, and said to the sea, 'Peace! Be still!' Then the wind ceased, and there was a dead calm. He said to them, 'Why are you afraid? Have you still no faith?' And they were filled with great awe and said to one another, 'Who then is this, that even the wind and the sea obey him?'

MARK 4:35–41

Prayer

Alone with none but you, my God,
I journey on my way.
What need I fear when you are near,
O King of night and day?
More safe am I within your hand
Than if a host did round me stand.[16]

Give me the courage to step out wherever you might call me, Lord, even if I cannot see where it leads. Amen

Saturday

The passion and commitment of the Celtic saints to both green and white martyrdom can be seen not only in their life stories, but also in the monastic Rules they wrote. The Rules of Columbanus, perhaps, are the most well-known and austere. Certainly, they are the most widespread across mainland Europe, especially what is now France, but also into Italy, where Columbanus died. As Katherine Lack suggests, 'When set down baldly in black and white, [the Rule of Columbanus] does not necessarily seem an attractive way of life.'[17] However, despite the austere and ascetic manner of the Rule, 'to the Franks it was heroic Christianity; it related directly to what they heard from the Bible, in a way that the existing continental church, so often urbane, established and rich, did not'.[18]

This 'heroic Christianity' was often what drew people to the faith and to the Celtic monastic centres. Taking direct influence and inspiration from the Desert Fathers and Mothers, who had left the urbanised and sanitised organisation of the new Roman/Latin church, the Celtic Christians knew that spiritual disciplines, both green and white martyrdom, were a way of life wholly dedicated to God. This was, perhaps, because the 'heroic' resonated deeply within the hearts and spirits of the Celtic people. The hero sagas and warrior spirit could be channelled into this passionate and strict form and expression of the Christian faith. As Esther De Waal says:

> In some indefinable way the heroic-age Celtic spirit was naturally predisposed to find something sympathetic in the stark asceticism and the extremism of the ideals of the Egyptian desert... Many monastic texts of this early period [such as the Stowe Missal and the Life of Columcille in the Book of Lismore]

commend [St Anthony of Egypt and St Paul of Thebes] as models. The monks of Brittany looked upon them as the first teachers of a life of solitary rigor… The lives of the saints… give many impressive accounts of these austerities, the austerity of the [monastic] site[s themselves] increased by their own self-inflicted austerities.[19]

The action of this heroic Christianity, for Columbanus, came from the idea of 'set[ting] your minds on things above, not on earthly things' (Colossians 3:2, NIV) and understanding God more clearly, or as Columbanus himself puts it in 'Sermon eight':

Unless we are filled with the urgent longing of heavenly desires, we shall necessarily be ensnared by earthly ones… So, since we are travellers and pilgrims in this world, let us think upon the end of the road that is our life, for the end of our way is our home… Many lose their true home because they have a greater love for the road that leads them there… Let us pray to him, for although he is invisible and unfathomable, God the Trinity is still known and present to us, according to the degree of our purity. Let us pray to him, I say, while we are here, so that there we may enter in more intimately and understand more clearly.[20]

It may be that the austerity of the Rules of Columbanus was a reflection of the importance he put on focusing on 'heavenly desires'.

So, when it comes to giving things up and living by spiritual disciplines, the Celtic saints are a great place to look for inspiration. Over the next week, we will look at what it might mean for us to live by a monastic Rule, or Way of Life, today.

Contemplation

Have you ever thought of living 'heroic' Christianity – living the kind of faith that those who gave everything up lived? Do you feel inspired perhaps to put a little more into 'being a Christian' after reading some of the stories from the past week? Think about how you live your Christian life, and if it could be a little 'more'.

Reading

So if you have been raised with Christ, seek the things that are above, where Christ is, seated at the right hand of God. Set your minds on things that are above, not on things that are on earth, for you have died, and your life is hidden with Christ in God. When Christ who is your life is revealed, then you also will be revealed with him in glory.

Put to death, therefore, whatever in you is earthly: fornication, impurity, passion, evil desire, and greed (which is idolatry). On account of these the wrath of God is coming on those who are disobedient. These are the ways you also once followed, when you were living that life. But now you must get rid of all such things – anger, wrath, malice, slander, and abusive language from your mouth. Do not lie to one another, seeing that you have stripped off the old self with its practices and have clothed yourselves with the new self, which is being renewed in knowledge according to the image of its creator.

COLOSSIANS 3:1–10

Prayer

Almighty God, King of kings and Lord of lords, draw me to a deeper and more real life in you and for you. May my belief not just be a religious label, but may the depth and commitment I have to you be seen in all that I do. Help me to strip off the old self and replace it with something 'more'. Amen

Contemplation
for the second Sunday in Lent

The Celtic Christians practised white martyrdom,
where they gave up all they knew of what
life was about for the sake of God.
How might you do this better?

Week two

Monday

Part of every monastic life is in keeping a Rule, or Way of Life, whether that is a calling to a First Order where one enters a monastery or convent, or whether it is to a Third Order or New Monastic community, where one lives as a lay person. This can even apply to someone out in the world and everyday life, but who commits to follow the Rule or Way of the order or community to which one has chosen to belong. This commitment to a Rule is, in itself, a type of sacrifice, a step into green martyrdom, and giving up one's own self-centred desires. It is a commitment to something greater than yourself, and to something more ancient than many of the new programmes which are available for personal discipleship.

The spiritual discipline of living by a Rule should not be a weight or burden on one's life but, as Thomas Merton said, a Rule is 'an exterior framework, a kind of scaffolding with which [one is] to help himself build up the spiritual structure of his own life with God'.[21]

The fourth-century British monk Morgan, better known by his Latin name Pelagius, said of a Rule:

> In a single day, we make so many decisions we cannot possibly weigh up the good and evil consequences of each decision. We are liable to make foolish and wrong decisions. For this reason, we need a rule, a simple set of moral principles that we can apply to each decision we make. This will not be foolproof, but with a good rule, our decision will far more often be right than wrong.
>
> Another reason for a rule is this: Jesus tells us to pray always; yet sometimes we love to devote much time to prayer

whereas at other times we are dry or feel far too busy to pray. A rule prevents us from making excuses; it spurs us to pray at a particular time even when our heart is cold toward God.[22]

Living by a Rule enables us simply to have a structure in our living, in our walk with God. It is like placing a garden trellis out for a plant; it does not hinder, but aids the growth, giving extra strength and support. This week, we will be looking at what it means to live by a Rule or Way of Life, to embody this green martyrdom. As we unfold the concept of living by a Rule, you might want to think about whether you wish to implement one into your own walk with God and for your own life, or even look at ones already followed by people in contemporary Christianity.

Contemplation

Have you ever felt like you needed or wanted something which would help you in how to live out your life as a Christian – something a little more structured than just trying to 'make it up as you go along' with some biblical understanding? What would it mean to you to have a framework to live your Christian life from?

Reading

The Lord spoke to Moses, saying: Speak to the Israelites and say to them: When either men or women make a special vow, the vow of a nazirite, to separate themselves to the Lord, they shall separate themselves from wine and strong drink; they shall drink no wine vinegar or other vinegar, and shall not drink any grape juice or eat grapes, fresh or dried. All their days as nazirites they shall eat nothing that is produced by the grape-vine, not even the seeds or the skins.

All the days of their nazirite vow no razor shall come upon the head; until the time is completed for which they separate themselves to the Lord, they shall be holy; they shall let the locks of the head grow long.

All the days that they separate themselves to the Lord they shall not go near a corpse. Even if their father or mother, brother or sister, should die, they may not defile themselves; because their consecration to God is upon the head. All their days as nazirites they are holy to the Lord.

If someone dies very suddenly nearby, defiling the consecrated head, then they shall shave the head on the day of their cleansing; on the seventh day they shall shave it. On the eighth day they shall bring two turtle-doves or two young pigeons to the priest at the entrance of the tent of meeting, and the priest shall offer one as a sin-offering and the other as a burnt-offering, and make atonement for them, because they incurred guilt by reason of the corpse. They shall sanctify the head that same day, and separate themselves to the Lord for their days as nazirites, and bring a male lamb a year old as a guilt-offering. The former time shall be void, because the consecrated head was defiled.

This is the law for the nazirites when the time of their consecration has been completed: they shall be brought to the entrance of the tent of meeting, and they shall offer their gift to the Lord, one male lamb a year old without blemish as a burnt-offering, one ewe lamb a year old without blemish as a sin-offering, one ram without blemish as an offering of well-being, and a basket of unleavened bread, cakes of choice flour mixed with oil and unleavened wafers spread with oil, with their grain-offering and their drink-offerings… This is the law for the nazirites who take a vow. Their offering to the Lord must be in accordance with the nazirite vow, apart from what else they can afford. In accordance with whatever vow they take, so they shall do, following the law for their consecration.
NUMBERS 6:1–15, 21

Prayer

God of all freedom, sometimes I need something to hold on to. Sometimes trying to find my way is hard. Help me to find the best way to frame my life with you, and help me to find something to aid growth in my faith. Amen

Tuesday

Numerous New Monastic communities, including the Community of Aidan and Hilda into which I am a vowed member, take their inspiration from Celtic monastic Rules for their own Rule, or Way of Life. These ancient Rules can be found in various places, one of which is a book called *The Celtic Monk*, in which Father Uinseann Ó Maidín collects nine different Irish monastic Rules, and some other writings. In the introduction to the book, Maidín tells us this:

> Irish secular life was based on the clan or family unity, with the father or chieftain at its head. Family ties, kinship and the personal rule of the leader of the group was the common bond, and any other approach would have been neither understood nor accepted by the people. For this reason monasticism, with its strong emphasis on community and an abbot at its head, was a concept the Irish could easily grasp and embrace.[23]

This was also true of the British Celts, who, according to Maidín, were the influence on Irish Christians with regards to monastic-style Christianity. He says:

> Saint Patrick, during the course of his ministry [though Christianity already existed in Ireland when he arrived], set up an ecclesiastical administration in which the diocese was paramount... When barbarian depredations put an end for a time to the influence of continental Europe on the Irish church, Irishmen turned their eyes to Britain for inspiration and guidance. Monastic life, traditionally held to have been imported from Egypt, flourished across the Irish Sea, and

Irish travellers quickly came under its influence. Saint Enda, after returning from Candida Casa (Whithorn) [in around 484], founded his monastery on Aran Mor, giving Ireland what was probably its first monastery.[24]

Enda is often referred to as the patriarch of Irish monasticism.

Having gained the influence of the British monasteries in the fifth century, it was the Irish missions which heavily influenced the conversion of the Anglo-Saxons and Picts in the sixth and seventh centuries to this Celtic monastic Christianity. The influence of this monastic life flowed back and forth between Britain and Ireland over the years, each influencing the other. What remained as a foundational aspect of all the interflow of inspiration was the dedication of the monks and nuns to the Rule of Life, to the spiritual disciplines of the Rule. This is also true of those who dedicate themselves to a Rule or Way of Life today in Third Order or New Monastic communities. This is still an important expression of the Christian faith to many modern 'lay' Christians.

Contemplation

As we travel on our Lenten journey, consider what influences have formed and forged the Christian life you live. What or who have been the main influences on you as you have grown and developed in your faith? How might you be inspired by the monastic way of being a Christian which has influenced so many over the centuries?

Reading

After staying there for a considerable time, Paul said farewell to the believers and sailed for Syria, accompanied by Priscilla and Aquila. At Cenchreae he had his hair cut, for he was under a [nazirite] vow...

'So, do what we tell you. We have four men who are under a [nazirite] vow. Join these men, go through the rite of purification with them, and pay for the shaving of their heads. Thus all will know that there is nothing in what they have been told about you, but that you yourself observe and guard the law. But as for the Gentiles who have become believers, we have sent a letter with our judgement that they should abstain from what has been sacrificed to idols and from blood and from what is strangled and from fornication.' Then Paul took the men, and the next day, having purified himself, he entered the temple with them, making public the completion of the days of purification when the sacrifice would be made for each of them.

ACTS 18:18; 21:23–26

Prayer

May the great saints of the past inspire and encourage me to live a great life for you, God. Amen

Wednesday

Part of the commitment to monastic Rules, whichever type they are, is to keep hours of prayer, to be committed to a rhythm of prayer throughout the day. Punctuating the day with moments of prayer and of stopping to focus on the divine presence is a major part of all monasticism, and historic Celtic monasticism was no exception. In numerous Celtic monastic sites and centres, a tall round tower can be seen – or the ruins of one. This tower had a few purposes, but one in particular was to be a bell tower to signal times of collective prayer. The rhythm of the day was important to the Celtic saints, as Thomas O'Loughlin says:

> Time was viewed as a background to an unfolding programme running from the moment of creation, the Alpha, to the moment of final consummation, the Omega, and the Christian's task was to know that Christ as Saviour was key to this programme, and then to fall into place with it so that the time-pattern of his or her own life was nowhere out of harmony with the divine metronome.[25]

Although most famous for writing the *Ecclesiastical History of the English*, the Venerable Bede also wrote other books. At the end of the *Ecclesiastical History*, he lists by name more than 77 books, including 57 Bible commentaries, which he wrote between the ages of 30 to 59. Three of these books are about time, or chronology, the largest of which is *The Reckoning of Time*. In this tome, Bede records the course of the moon and seasons, as well as the different months according to the different cultures which had inhabited Britain. In fact, it is to this book that we owe a great deal of our knowledge of the festivals of ancient Britain. Time is important. Time is part of the divine rhythm of the universe, and we are to fall into place with this rhythm, so that we are in time with the 'divine metronome'.

So, for the Celtic saints, time was not something to be used or indeed wasted lightly; it was a divine gift and was part of the unfolding plan, the rhythm of the universe. The use of time was significant, and the keeping of hours of prayer played a significant role. This did not mean that prayer at other times was not practised – the lives of the saints show this – but the deliberate hours which punctuate the day were significant, like a deliberate oasis in the flow of the day, set aside for refreshing (even when we don't feel like it!).

Contemplation

How do you use your time? How do you even see and understand time? Is it a gift from God? Have you ever considered that you are a part of a divine flow and rhythm which has been going since the beginning of time? How might you better organise your time so that you always have time to spend in stillness and prayer with God?

Reading

And God said, 'Let there be lights in the dome of the sky to separate the day from the night; and let them be for signs and for seasons and for days and years, and let them be lights in the dome of the sky to give light upon the earth.' And it was so.
GENESIS 1:14–15

One day Peter and John were going up to the temple at the hour of prayer, at three o'clock in the afternoon. And a man lame from birth was being carried in. People would lay him daily at the gate of the temple called the Beautiful Gate so that he could ask for alms from those entering the temple.
ACTS 3:1–2

Prayer

Holy one, instigator of time itself, help me to place a rhythm into each day which includes times of prayer. May I make better use of my time, doing less and being more, and drawing closer to you. Amen

Thursday

There are numerous books available on living by a Rule or Way of Life. Today and tomorrow, we will look at two books, one each day, written on living by the Way of Life of the Community of Aidan and Hilda, a globally dispersed, Celtic-inspired New Monastic community.[26] Today we will look briefly at *Followers of the Way: Ancient discipleship for modern Christians* by Simon Reed (BRF, 2017).[27]

This book, which follows on from the author's *Creating Community*,[28] is about what it means to live by a Rule of Life in our modern world, and how it is helpful towards lifelong discipleship. As Reed says:

> I've come to believe that [a Rule of Life is] absolutely vital and essential to the process of truly realising what it is to be a disciple of Jesus… If you want to go on a journey, you need a map. If you want to make a cake, you need a recipe. If you want to build a house, you need a plan. It's exactly the same with being a disciple of Jesus. We need to know what we are trying to do, how to get there, and how to measure our progress along the way.[29]

A Rule of Life helps us to plan out what it is we want to do in our walk with Christ, and how we might achieve that. This idea of framing our lifelong discipleship on a Rule of Life, as set out in *Followers of the Way*, helps us to realise the achievability of our spiritual goals and aspirations or, perhaps more importantly, helps us to see what goals we set ourselves which may be unachievable. Most people are pretty good at setting themselves unachievable goals!

Followers of the Way is an excellent practical guide to how we might live out this way of discipleship in our modern context, and why it is helpful and important. The Rule was the foundation of Celtic, and all other, monasticism. You might wonder, then, why the term Way or Rule of Life isn't found in the Bible. As Simon Reed says, 'Rather like the Trinity, the word itself is not there, but the idea very much is.'[30]

So, if the idea of living by a Rule is clearly found in scripture, including the New Testament, even if the word is not there, why are more Christians not using this form of daily focus for their lifelong discipleship of being an active follower of Christ as they are being transformed by divine grace?

Contemplation

How might living by a Rule or Way of Life help in your discipleship as a Christian? If it has been such a help to so many from our spiritual heritage, how might it help you as you live your life as a disciple of Christ?

Reading

> And Jesus came and said to them, 'All authority in heaven and on earth has been given to me. Go therefore and make disciples of all nations, baptising them in the name of the Father and of the Son and of the Holy Spirit, and teaching them to obey everything that I have commanded you. And remember, I am with you always, to the end of the age.'
>
> MATTHEW 28:18–20

Prayer

Jesus, as I learn more of what it means to follow you, to be your disciple, help me to find a way to structure my life which will bring me closer to you and make me more like you. Amen

Friday

Yesterday, we looked at one book written about living by a Rule of Life based on the Way of Life of the Community of Aidan and Hilda, and today we will be looking at another. Today we will look at *A Pilgrim Way: New Celtic Monasticism for everyday people* by Ray Simpson (Kevin Mayhew, 2005).[31] This book is both the story of how the community began and an expansion on each of the elements of the Way of Life that all the members live by. It shows why each point was chosen and has practical examples of how various members live it out differently.

In reference to why this way of living might be relevant to the modern Christian, Simpson says:

> People look for a path that is simple yet not simplistic; in an age of mobility, people look for roots; in an age of dislocation, people want to reconnect with the whole. An authentic Way, such as is offered [by the Community of Aidan and Hilda], does not stifle our personality, it frees us to live from our deepest core… To live authentically means that I choose my lifestyle, I do not succumb to the lifestyle others foist upon me. It means that I use my time, money and talents according to my deepest convictions.[32]

The means by which the Way of Life of this particular community is lived out is organic and each member is able to create their own life-giving expression of the Rule so that it best fits their circumstances. This does not make it 'floaty' in any way, but gives a framework for free growth, just like a garden plant growing against a trellis. The roots of the plant are firm (that is, the person is rooted and established in Christ), and the chosen 'trellis' is set (that is, the general expression – in the case of the Community of Aidan and Hilda, this is Celtic-inspired Christianity), but the growth itself will be different for each plant. Every version of the same plant, for example, looks different; though every one of them is the same genus and their essence is the same, the plants themselves each have their own characteristics, or perhaps even personalities, and growth patterns depending upon soil type, light, wind direction, etc.

In fact, it has been suggested that the two words 'rule' and 'trellis' come from the same root. In a book looking at the Rule of Saint Benedict, the writer says:

> The root meaning of the Latin and Greek words translated as 'rule' is *trellis*. Saint Benedict was not promulgating rules for living; he was establishing a framework on which a life can grow. While a branch of a plant climbing a trellis cannot go in any direction it wants, you cannot know in advance just which way it will go. The plant is finding its own path within a structure.[33]

Simpson continues with this same idea in *A Pilgrim Way* when he says, 'A common Way of Life provides general principles and elements. A personal Rule applies those to one's own circumstances.'[34]

So we can take on a Rule created by a monastic group such as the Community of Aidan and Hilda, but we express it in our own unique, individual way. The purpose of it is to give a framework to our own personal growth to help bring life to who we are and what we become in our life's journey with God. This means that living by a Rule, or committing to this particular spiritual discipline, is not akin to tying ourselves down again to something like the Torah; it is, in fact, taking the essence of why God shaped the relationship in the first place around a framework and living freely from it. We must understand that this framework is for our benefit, not for our binding.

Contemplation

Have you ever thought about a Rule or Way of Life as a trellis, something upon which you could frame your growth and walk with God? In what ways are we like a plant with or without a trellis?

How might such a thing help you to be better as you grow as a Christian?

Reading

One sabbath [Jesus] was going through the cornfields; and as they made their way his disciples began to pluck heads of grain. The Pharisees said to him, 'Look, why are they doing what is not lawful on the sabbath?' And he said to them, 'Have you never read what David did when he and his companions were hungry and in need of food? He entered the house of God, when Abiathar was high priest, and ate the bread of the Presence, which it is not lawful for any but the priests to eat, and he gave some to his companions.' Then he said to them, 'The sabbath was made for humankind, and not humankind for the sabbath; so the Son of Man is lord even of the sabbath.'

MARK 2:23–28

Prayer

Holy and loving one, as we grow in you, may we know the freedom which comes from our own personalities which you have given us. Guide me to know what to use as a framework for my growth, to aid me and give me strength in you. Amen

Saturday

Over the past week, we have looked at various perspectives of living by a Rule or Way of Life. We have seen ancient and modern Celtic views and seen how and why this can be a helpful way of living. This is, of course, all about the green and white martyrdoms which we have been looking at since Ash Wednesday. It is particularly relevant to those who have decided to give things up for Lent and sacrifice something as a way of remembering the sacrifice of Christ so that we can be drawn closer to the divine by means of a spiritual discipline. A natural expansion of this Lenten practice is to commit to live by a Rule of Life every day.

Living by a Rule is all about giving our whole lives over to the spiritual disciplines which go along with it, not just a little bit of our lives for the weeks of Lent. We give up our ideas of how best to live our life and we live a more structured one based on the framework of a monastic Rule. This is an ancient way of expressing one's dedication to the Christian life, one which millions of Christians have benefited from since the Desert Fathers and Mothers and the birth of monasticism, including thousands who are part of monastic orders or New Monastic communities today. But those weren't the first Ways of Life written for Christians.

When we looked at the book *Followers of the Way*, we mentioned that even though the term 'Rule' or 'Way of Life' is not mentioned in scripture, the concept is there. One of the other ways in which we know that this concept was part of the early church is a very early set of instructions called the Didache. The Didache is one of the earliest Christian documents, predating a number of the writings which make up the New Testament. It is presented, not as doctrine or teaching, but as a *way of life* for those who wish to follow Christ. 'Didache' is a Greek word which means training or teaching. As Thomas O'Loughlin puts it in *The Didache: A window on the earliest Christians*, it is the 'lifestyle that has to be imbedded in one's life if one is to live as a disciple'.[35] It is arguably the earliest 'Way of Life' document for followers of Christ. O'Loughlin also tells us:

> If you have heard the good news, now you must make it a part of your life. We today make a distinction between 'discipleship' and 'discipline'; the first is a lifelong endeavour, the second is rules and regulations. For the early Christians, there was no such division: the Didache was concerned with the discipline – if you knew its demands, you were on the Way because this was what a disciple manifested.[36]

This non-distinction between 'discipline' and 'discipleship' may be a difficult concept for us to understand. Discipline can often be viewed with a negative connotation due to the usage of the word in such places as education systems, or even within our own homes when a parent disciplines a child. But this is not only what discipline is; it is also the keeping of a routine and regime, like a fitness regime. This idea is found in the Didache, where discipline is that which helps the disciple learn how to live a life like Christ. When it comes to a way of life set out as in the Didache, O'Loughlin comments, 'The rules were not there just as an ethical standard: they were there as part of a formal relationship with God... [The rules] presuppose a relationship.'[37]

This is what it means to be 'Christ-like' and to be 'Christian', as when the apostle Paul writes to the Christians in the church in Corinth and says, 'As the Spirit of the Lord works within us, we become more and more like him and reflect his glory even more' (2 Corinthians 3:18, TLB). So discipleship for the early church was a gradual, lifelong transformation of the person through the work of God within them into something more like Christ, and this was lived out through following a Way of Life, like the Didache.

Contemplation

How do you view 'discipline' and 'discipleship'? Is discipline just a negative term that relates to being told off? Are they different things or are they interwoven, or even the same? How might the concept of them being the same or interwoven change the way you view spiritual disciplines, such as living by a Rule or Way of Life?

Reading

The Way of Life: There are two Ways, a Way of Life and a Way of Death, and the difference between these two Ways is great. The Way of Life is this: Thou shalt love first the Lord thy Creator, and secondly thy neighbour as thyself; and thou shalt do nothing to any man that thou wouldst not wish to be done to thyself...

Never give way to anger, for anger leads to murder. Likewise refrain from fanaticism, quarrelling, and hot-temperedness, for these too can breed murder...

Take care that nobody tempts you away from the path of this [Way], for such a man's tuition can have nothing to do with God. If you can shoulder the Lord's yoke in its entirety, then you will be perfect; but if that is too much for you, do as much as you can.

The Didache: from parts 1, 3 and 6[38]

Prayer

Loving God, you have always known that giving us guidelines is the best way for us to get the most out of our relationship with you. May I know the benefit of a disciplined way of life, and be committed to putting this into place for you. Amen

Contemplation
for the third **Sunday** in Lent

What would it mean to live by a monastic Rule?
If you already live by one, what could you do to
enhance its effect on your walk with God?

Week three

Monday

Storytelling has long been a part of our humanity.[39] Ever since we could communicate, we have in all likelihood been telling stories to one another; certainly for thousands of years, stories have been told and collected, orally and through writing. Stories, poems and songs help us to make sense of the world. Through them, we begin to fathom who we are, where we have come from and where we might go from here. They enable us to learn from our past so that we can better step into the future. They allow us to be inspired by people who came before us through hero sagas and true-life accounts. Many of the greatest spiritual teachers through the ages have used storytelling as a way of getting across truths so deep they may be impossible to put into words. Jesus used allegory and illustrations from real life to express and expand his message. The ancient Celts, like many cultures, loved stories. There was an ancient Celtic tradition which today is known as 'passing of the harp,' where communities would gather in the Mead Hall, or other communal hall, and tell stories through the evenings around a fire, with food and drink flowing.

This tradition was continued in the Celtic monastic communities, such as the one in Whitby, where Bede makes mention of it in his *Ecclesiastical History of the English People*. The key figure in this passage by Bede is Cædmon, who brought to life Bible stories and told them in the common language of the ordinary Angle folk. Accounts of saints' lives were also popular among the early Celtic Christians, as well as the songs, prayers and poems which they wrote. What these things do is deepen and bring to life that which is often intangible; it connects deep truths with ordinary lives to make those lives extraordinary. The medium of storytelling may have changed over the years – from the oral tradition with the passing of the harp to written stories in books, to movies and television programmes, and now in various digital formats – but the stories themselves are as important to our culture as ever. Storytelling is within our DNA, a part of who we are as human beings.

We have already had some life stories of Celtic saints, so this week we will be looking at some prayers, poems and creative expressions of the Celtic Christians which relate to our journey through Lent. These writings have been inspiring Christians for hundreds of years. Allow the divine flow of this inspiration to penetrate your deepest essence; let it seep into the very core of your being and just see what happens.

Contemplation

Which stories or creative writings, such as poetry or songs, inspire you? Draw to mind that which inspires you most. Watch it, read it or listen to it now.

Reading

Give ear, O my people, to my teaching;
    incline your ears to the words of my mouth.
I will open my mouth in a parable;
    I will utter dark sayings from of old,
things that we have heard and known,
    that our ancestors have told us.
We will not hide them from their children;
    we will tell to the coming generation
the glorious deeds of the Lord, and his might,
    and the wonders that he has done.
PSALM 78:1–4

Prayer

Creator God, you not only created the world which we see, but you created creativity itself! Thank you for the creative spirit within humanity. Thank you for all that has inspired me so far in life. May I learn to harness the creativity which you have placed within me and express it as part of my spiritual path. Amen

Tuesday

Patrick's breastplate is arguably the best known of the Lorica prayers, the prayers of protection, or the Breastplate prayers. There are two famous translations of Patrick's breastplate: Kuno Meyer's translation which starts, 'I arise today through a mighty strength, the invocation of the Trinity'; and C.F. Alexander's translation which starts, 'I bind unto myself today the strong name of the Trinity'. This hymn is one which calls on God and heavenly powers for protection against all types of evil and negativity, both spiritual and from other people.

The Celtic saints believed in the power of God to protect them. It was as real to them as the sword and shield at the side of a soldier. David Adam says that this prayer attributed to Patrick:

> … expresses so well much of the early Celtic Christian faith. It vibrates still with the God who surrounds us, the Christ who is with us and the Spirit within us. In these three affirmations, the Divine Glory is woven into all life like a fine thread; there is a presence and power that pervades everything.[40]

This sense of the power and protection of God surrounding the Celtic saints may perhaps be related to the fact that they understood the work of the cross not simply as the substitutionary atonement, in the way that modern churches do; instead, the main teaching of the work of the cross at that time, it is thought, was the *Christus Victor* theology. We will look at this more closely later on in our Lenten journey.

This understanding, however, meant that at the very core of the Celtic theology of the cross of Christ was the fact that the power of evil and of the devil was defeated and overcome. This meant that the power of God was ultimate over evil, and so could protect each person from harm outside God's will in the everyday. These Breastplate prayers, then, were a way in which the Celtic saints would cover themselves, verbally, in divine protection. They were a verbal reminder of the power of Christ through the cross over all evil. Words have power, and these words carried the power of God and the cross of Christ.

In C.F. Alexander's translation, there is the following stanza which exemplifies this:

Against all Satan's spells and wiles,
Against false words of heresy,
Against the knowledge that defiles,
Against the heart's idolatry,
Against the wizard's evil craft,
Against the death-wound and the burning,
The choking wave and poisoned shaft,
Protect me, Christ, till thy returning.[41]

Prayers of protection seem to be distinctly missing from today's prayer collections. Perhaps we place more faith in the practical world around us to protect us than the spiritual. Perhaps we have more faith in technology and the protection it offers us, with CCTV and other things which 'cover' us and watch over us, than we do in the power and presence of God pervading everything. Perhaps these prayers and this understanding need to become more prominent in our understanding of the work of the cross, and more interwoven within our lives each day.

Contemplation

How do you understand the concept of divine protection? Have you ever prayed specifically for divine protection? What about having a specific prayer to use? We have prayers which we repeat regularly for specific things which we have learned off by heart, whether that be the Lord's Prayer or grace before meals. What about learning all or part of a Lorica prayer?

Reading

The Lord answer you in the day of trouble!
   The name of the God of Jacob protect you!
May he send you help from the sanctuary,
   and give you support from Zion.
May he remember all your offerings,
   and regard with favour your burnt sacrifices.

May he grant you your heart's desire,
   and fulfil all your plans.
May we shout for joy over your victory,
   and in the name of our God set up our banners.
May the Lord fulfil all your petitions.

Now I know that the Lord will help his anointed;
   he will answer him from his holy heaven
   with mighty victories by his right hand.
Some take pride in chariots, and some in horses,
   but our pride is in the name of the Lord our God.
They will collapse and fall,
   but we shall rise and stand upright.

Give victory to the king, O Lord;
   answer us when we call.
PSALM 20

Prayer

Christ be with me, Christ within me, Christ behind me, Christ before me, Christ beside me, Christ to win me, Christ to comfort and restore me, Christ beneath me, Christ above me, Christ in quiet, Christ in danger, Christ in hearts of all that love me, Christ in mouth of friend and stranger.

I bind unto myself the name, the strong name of the Trinity; by invocation of the same, the Three in One, the One in Three, of whom all nature hath creation, Eternal Father, Spirit, Word: Praise to the Lord of my salvation, salvation is of Christ the Lord.[42]

Wednesday

Arguably the most famous ancient Celtic hymn today is 'Be thou my vision', which comes from Ireland and is most commonly dated around the eighth or ninth century, though some believe that it has an earlier date than that. It is thought that the early Irish saint and poet Dallán, also known as Eochaid mac Colla, who died in around 598, may have been the writer of some early form of this hymn, and the words have been chanted by monks from that time onwards. Although we know it best from the version often sung in churches today, versified as a hymn by Eleanor Hull (1860–1935),[43] the original, more literal, translation from which the versified version was taken was written by Mary Byrne (1880–1931). It is from Byrne's translation that I want to take some thoughts today.

In Byrne's translation, we can more clearly see the biblical inspiration for this ancient poem. In lines such as 'Be thou my meditation by day and night: may it be thou that I behold for ever in my sleep', and 'Be thou a shelter, be thou my stronghold: mayest thou raise me up in the company of angels',[44] we can hear echoes of the words of the psalmists of the Old Testament. This ancient Irish psalm, as we might call it, was, as many psalms of the Bible are, a cry to God for protection and guidance. The term 'Be thou' can be understood as quite a firm statement of 'God, you be…'. Imagine someone who is blind taking hold of the shoulder of someone who can see and saying, 'You be my eyes as we walk', 'Be thou my eyes'. This is the essence of the term 'Be thou' in this hymn. We are, as it were, taking hold of God and putting our whole trust in the divine leading.

This leading is not just in our vision, though, whether physical or of our inner leading but, as Byrne goes on to say, 'Be thou my speech' and 'understanding'. This hymn incorporates the whole being, *our* whole being, our vision, our speech, our understanding, all that we are, echoing the Celtic concept of non-duality in their spiritual understanding – everything was spiritual for them – no separation between sacred and secular, physical and spiritual. God, be thou my vision, my meditation/thought, my speech, my understanding/wisdom. Byrne also translates one line to say, 'Be thou my kingdom in heaven and earth', where we can see the echoes of the Lord's Prayer, and the desire that the divine kingdom will come in us and in the world. This kingdom can come in us and the world as a result of the work of the cross of Christ.

One final line from Byrne's translation takes us once again to the spiritual battle, a line which made it into the versified version: 'Be thou my battle-shield, be thou my sword'. Once again, this idea of spiritual battle, the defeat of the evil one and the overcoming power of God through Christ raises its head in Celtic poetry. This leads us to one final thought for today, the final connection of this hymn to ancient Celtic history: the tune we all sing it to. The tune itself is not that old, but the inspiration for the tune has history. The tune that 'Be thou my vision' is sung to, in whatever beat you play it, is the Irish folk tune 'Slane'. The name for this tune was taken from the Irish hill 'Slane', in County Meath. It was atop Slane Hill that Patrick lit his fire on Easter Sunday morning in 433 in defiance of the pagan High King, Loegaire, which ultimately led to Patrick having freedom to preach the gospel across all Ireland.[45]

So, when we sing this wonderful ancient Irish hymn, we are not only drawing on the words from the Celtic faith, but we are also remembering the faith of Patrick as he stood against the High King for the sake of Christ on Easter Sunday morning – the faith of Patrick and the other Celtic saints that the power of Christ is stronger than all other powers.

Contemplation

Who is God to you? Have you ever really thought about it? If you were going to write a verse to this poem/hymn, what would follow your 'Be thou' statements? Perhaps write some now.

Reading

I lift up my eyes to the hills –
　　from where will my help come?
My help comes from the Lord,
　　who made heaven and earth.
He will not let your foot be moved;
　　he who keeps you will not slumber.
He who keeps Israel
　　will neither slumber nor sleep.
The Lord is your keeper;
　　The Lord is your shade at your right hand.
The sun shall not strike you by day,
　　nor the moon by night.
The Lord will keep you from all evil;
　　he will keep your life.
The Lord will keep
　　your going out and your coming in
　　from this time on and forevermore.

PSALM 121

Prayer

High King of heaven, thou heaven's bright Sun,
O grant me its joys after vict'ry is won.
Great heart of my own heart, whatever befall,
still be though my vision, thou Ruler of all.[46]

Thursday

It wasn't until the middle of the seventh century that any of the Bible was written down in the English language, that is, the language of the Angles. Scripture was written in Latin, when it was written at all, although it would have been spoken in the native language so that the people would be able to understand it. We are told that, when Aidan began his mission to the Northumbrian Angles, the king, Oswald, acted as interpreter; when Aidan quoted scriptures in his Irish tongue, Oswald would have repeated them in the language of the Angles. But it was Cædmon who first *wrote down* any scripture in the native tongue of the Angles – what we now call Old English. Cædmon's life began as a cowherd in the monastic community in Whitby,[47] but in his dreams he was divinely gifted with songs based on scripture. Only one fragment of one song remains available to us today, part of his first dream about the creation story, which is also the earliest ever recorded poem written in the English language, and it is this:

> *Now must we honour heaven's guardian,*
> *the Measurer's might and his spirit's thought,*
> *the work of the wonder-Father, the eternal Lord,*
> *how he set a start of every marvel.*
> *He first fashioned heaven as a roof*
> *for the children of the earth, the holy Creator.*
> *Then mankind's Guardian afterward made*
> *middle earth, the eternal Lord,*
> *the land for men, the almighty Leader.*[48]

In this short extract of the poem, God is termed in seven different ways (a number which denoted spiritual perfection in Jewish spirituality): heaven's guardian, the measurer, the wonder-Father, eternal Lord, holy Creator, mankind's guardian and almighty leader. There is a reflection here of the Old Testament Jewish tradition of giving varying focuses to God by the particular name which is used. Each name draws a slightly different context to our understanding and view of God. We perhaps might picture God in different ways simply because of the different names given.

You may also notice, of course, the name Cædmon gives to this world upon which we live: 'middle earth', a not uncommon term in early medieval poems and songs such as this one. This is most likely to have been the inspiration for the name which J.R.R. Tolkien gave the world he created, inhabited by hobbits and dwarves and other fantastical things. This is the earth, which is in the middle between heaven and hell, the natural creation caught between light and dark, between good and evil. We can feel, just by unpacking that name a little, the tension we face in the natural realm, the pull within us between the light and the dark.

The reason this poem is included here in this journey towards Lent is because the Celtic Christians had the understanding that the whole of creation was being reconciled back to God through the work of Christ on the cross. It wasn't just humanity, but the work of the cross was the work to reconcile all things back to God – all of, and on, this middle earth.

This extract of Cædmon's poem is about the creation of the world, and it shows the great love which God has for the creation. As we journey towards resurrection, let us not forget that it is because God so loved the whole *world*, all of creation, not just humanity, that he gave his only Son (John 3:16). Let us remember the earth and how it groans as it waits to be reconciled with its Creator through the work of the cross of Christ (Romans 8:19–21).

Contemplation

How do you view the earth? Do you perceive it as something special and sacred? Or is it just where you live, just a place for you to be? How might you become more aware of the sacredness of the natural world around you?

Reading

In the beginning when God created the heavens and the earth, the earth was a formless void and darkness covered the face of the deep, while a wind from God swept over the face of the waters. Then God said, 'Let there be light'; and there was light. And God saw that the light was good; and God separated the light from the darkness. God called the light Day, and the darkness he called Night. And there was evening and there was morning, the first day.

And God said, 'Let there be a dome in the midst of the waters, and let it separate the waters from the waters.' So God made the dome and separated the waters that were under the dome from the waters that were above the dome. And it was so. God called the dome Sky. And there was evening and there was morning, the second day.

And God said, 'Let the waters under the sky be gathered together into one place, and let the dry land appear.' And it was so. God called the dry land Earth, and the waters that were gathered together he called Seas. And God saw that it was good. Then God said, 'Let the earth put forth vegetation: plants yielding seed, and fruit trees of every kind on earth that bear fruit with the seed in it.' And it was so. The earth brought forth vegetation: plants yielding seed of every kind, and trees of every kind bearing fruit with the seed in it. And God saw that it was good. And there was evening and there was morning, the third day.

And God said, 'Let there be lights in the dome of the sky to separate the day from the night; and let them be for signs and for seasons and for days and years, and let them be lights in the dome of the sky to give light upon the earth.' And it was so. God made the two great lights – the greater light to rule the day and the lesser light to rule the night – and the stars. God set them in the dome of the sky to give light upon the earth, to rule over the day and over the night, and to separate the light from the darkness. And God saw that it was good. And there was evening and there was morning, the fourth day.

And God said, 'Let the waters bring forth swarms of living creatures, and let birds fly above the earth across the dome of the sky.' So God created the great sea monsters and every living creature that moves, of every kind, with which the waters swarm, and every winged bird of every kind. And God saw that it was good. God blessed them, saying, 'Be fruitful and multiply and fill the waters in the seas, and let birds multiply on the earth.' And there was evening and there was morning, the fifth day.

And God said, 'Let the earth bring forth living creatures of every kind: cattle and creeping things and wild animals of the earth of every kind.' And it was so. God made the wild animals of the earth of every kind, and the cattle of every kind, and everything that creeps upon the ground of every kind. And God saw that it was good.

Then God said, 'Let us make humankind in our image, according to our likeness; and let them have dominion over the fish of the sea, and over the birds of the air, and over the cattle, and over all the wild animals of the earth, and over every creeping thing that creeps upon the earth.'

So God created humankind in his image, in the image of God he created them; male and female he created them.

GENESIS 1:1–27

Prayer

Thank you, Almighty God, for the beauty which we can see in this middle earth. Thank you that we can connect with you through it. Help us to perceive the sacredness of the earth more and more as we care for it and live as a part of the whole creation. Amen

Friday

Somewhere in the late 800s to early 900s, a Welsh poem came into being called 'Praise to God', in which 'there is a great emphasis on the saving *action* of God. On his victory, "triumph" and "honour" as well as his largesse.'[49] In the poem, 'Christ is depicted as a conquering hero, and the text consciously imitates the language of the secular heroic tradition'.[50] This poem also holds a great deal of eucharistic language, such as 'Through the cross, blood-stained, came salvation to the world.'[51] All of these things root this poem deeply in the message of the cross of Christ and give it high merit to be included in our Lenten journey.

The idea that Christ went to the cross and came from it as a conquering hero akin to the heroes in the great Celtic and Anglo-Saxon sagas can be seen in numerous Celtic hymns and poems, the most famous of which, *The Dream of the Rood*, will come up in Holy Week. However, this Welsh poem, 'Praise to God', is another example of it. The poem speaks of the triumph of God's love, who will free us on judgement day and lead us to the feast in paradise in the pure release from the burden of sin.

As I hope we are beginning to see from the past few days looking at some of the hymns and poems of the Celtic Christians, the idea of the victory of Christ over evil and sin was very strong in the theology of the Celtic Christians. Hero sagas were important to the Celtic and Anglo-Saxon people. They were the way in which great warriors were not only remembered but honoured. They would sing of great feats and valour; of the struggles the hero went through, and quite often there would be a reason that the hero went through this struggle, often as a sacrificial giving to save someone or some group of people.

In this way, the hero was not only held in high esteem by the people, but they would also be held worthy by God, or the gods, depending upon whether this was a Christian tale or not.

This hero status was placed upon Christ and the cross was seen as a battleground with the most ancient of foes – the devil. The title of the poem we have referred to today – 'Praise to God' – states right at the start who has won the victory in this epic battle. Christ is the conquering hero, and we can stand in that victory with him, and we can also bring our praise to God!

Contemplation

Have you ever considered Christ as a conquering hero? Have you ever come across this concept of the work of the cross? What difference might it make to the way you view not just the work of the cross, but what it means to you in your daily life if you understood it this way?

Reading

And war broke out in heaven; Michael and his angels fought against the dragon. The dragon and his angels fought back, but they were defeated, and there was no longer any place for them in heaven. The great dragon was thrown down, that ancient serpent, who is called the Devil and Satan, the deceiver of the whole world – he was thrown down to the earth, and his angels were thrown down with him.

Then I heard a loud voice in heaven, proclaiming,

'Now have come the salvation and the power
    and the kingdom of our God
    and the authority of his Messiah,
for the accuser of our comrades has been thrown down,
    who accuses them day and night before our God.

But they have conquered him by the blood of the Lamb
and by the word of their testimony,
for they did not cling to life even in the face of death.
Rejoice then, you heavens
and those who dwell in them!
But woe to the earth and the sea,
for the devil has come down to you
with great wrath,
because he knows that his time is short!'

REVELATION 12:7–12

Prayer

Great and mighty God, thank you for all you have done in the battle against evil. Thank you for the work of the cross and how this means that you have overcome the 'prince of this world',[52] and that I can live in that victory. Help me to see what that really means for my daily life. Amen

Saturday

Our final Celtic poem for this week is simply entitled 'Prayer', and is attributed to Ciaran of Clonmacnoise but, as is the case with many of these prayers, is likely to have been written a little while after his time. This prayer – the first line of which is in Latin, the rest in Irish – is a prayer for forgiveness, which is why it is here at the end of the week. It does keep the theme of the hero saga, ending with the line 'O rock-like warrior of a hundred hosts, O fair crowned one, victorious, skilled in battle, forgive'.[53]

This poem, or prayer, gives wonderful names to Christ as it seeks forgiveness: names such as 'guiding light', 'holy storyteller', 'holy scholar', 'silent one' and 'generous and thunderous giver of gifts'. Perhaps the names were attributed as direct statements to the sins of the writer. Perhaps, for example, he felt he had been blinded by something, or was struggling in the darkness, and so needed a 'guiding light', or perhaps he needed some guidance or advice from the holy scholar and holy storyteller. Let's not forget that bards were held in very high esteem in Ireland at this time; they were the ones who held the sacred stories and were entrusted to pass them on to others. Christ here *is* that holy scholar and holy storyteller.

This ancient Irish poem is similar to the more well-known, and slightly shorter, prayer known as 'The Jesus prayer', in which the one praying asks for Jesus to have mercy upon them after naming Christ as 'Son of God'. This Irish extended version has a very similar feel, naming Christ and then finishing every stanza with simply – 'Forgive'. The depth of the request of the Mighty Victorious Warrior Jesus Christ to forgive in this ancient prayer can be felt in its words and style.

Of course, the subject of forgiveness is at the heart of the work of the cross, and it is the season of Lent through which we really begin to gain a sense of the depth of forgiveness that the cross of Christ brings. So often, though, we are quite broad and vague about our forgiveness or within our confessions. Here, in this poem/prayer, the author brings in attributes of Christ which could well be related to what he is asking forgiveness for. What an interesting concept! The Jewish people used different names for God throughout their scriptures (what we call the Old Testament) to draw out the essence behind what they were focusing on; whether that be *El Elyon* (God of gods), *YHWH Rapha* (God who heals) or *YHWH Mekoddishkem* (God who sanctifies), the specific characteristic of God was focused upon. Maybe we need to be more specific in both what we are asking forgiveness for, and which particular characteristic of God/Christ that might be related to. And, just like the author of this Celtic prayer for forgiveness, we don't have to stick with just the names which are used in scripture, which were, of course, first used by people creating them for just this sort of purpose.

Contemplation

Which divine attributes most resonate with you at this point on your life journey? Which aspects of the divine nature do you most need at this time. When you pray or commune with God, do you always just use 'God' or 'Lord', or do you speak more specifically in relation to what you are asking for or praying about? Why not begin to expand upon the terms and names you use for God in your prayers?

Reading

But Peter, standing with the eleven, raised his voice and addressed them, 'Men of Judea and all who live in Jerusalem, let this be known to you, and listen to what I say. Indeed, these are not drunk, as you suppose, for it is only nine o'clock in the morning. No, this is what was spoken through the prophet Joel:

'In the last days it will be, God declares, that I will pour out my Spirit upon all flesh, and your sons and your daughters shall prophesy, and your young men shall see visions, and your old men shall dream dreams…'

Now when they heard this, they were cut to the heart and said to Peter and to the other apostles, 'Brothers, what should we do?' Peter said to them, 'Repent, and be baptised every one of you in the name of Jesus Christ so that your sins may be forgiven; and you will receive the gift of the Holy Spirit. For the promise is for you, for your children, and for all who are far away, everyone whom the Lord our God calls to him.'

ACTS 2:14–17, 37–39

Prayer

Mighty Victorious Warrior Jesus Christ:

O star-like sun,
O guiding Light
O home of the planets,
O fiery-maned and marvellous one,
O fertile, undulating, fiery-sea,
Forgive

O overflowing, loving, silent one,
O generous and thunderous giver of gifts,
Forgive.[54]

Contemplation
for the fourth **Sunday** in Lent

The words we use in our spiritual acts
and services are powerful.
Spend time contemplating how you use words
in these times and how you might better use them.

Week four

Monday

Celtic Christians saw the divine in every aspect of life; there were no dualistic concepts for the Celtic people, and everything was spiritual. As they went on journeys, they would be aware that the divine presence was not just in them, but with them, and also in everything around them and in everyone that they encountered. But even more than this, they believed that the divine was flowing through everything so that what we might call 'divine appointments' weren't a surprise, but an expectation. It was God's desire to set up opportunities for them to share the gospel or allow the divine power to flow through them in miraculous ways.

A journey wasn't just to get from one place to another; it was a transitional period in which God was present. This was true in their physical journeys as well as their concept of their life journey, and their journeys leading up to such things as Lent, the journey we are currently on together.

As someone who tries to embody, in my modern context, the heart and attitude of Celtic Christian spirituality, I try to keep this in mind when I travel around physically. There was one such occasion which I would like to share with you.

I was on a train journey between London and Lindisfarne at a table seat. I was sitting the aisle side, and a young man was sitting near the window. He obviously worked in some kind of technology role as he was surrounded by devices and was 'pinging' emails and information here, there and everywhere. He was totally absorbed in what he was doing, talking on the phone, using his laptop, texting and sifting through data on a tablet all at the same time. As you can imagine, London to Lindisfarne is not a quick pop around the corner, and it wasn't long until his devices began to fail him. His tablet battery died, the signal dropped out on the phone as the train hurtled along the tracks in and out of pockets of signal, the Wi-Fi on the train wasn't fast enough for him and his laptop struggled, so he began to get more and more frustrated. In the end, he gave up, sat back in his seat with a sigh and, with almost visible exasperation on his face, resorted to what seemed to be a totally alien concept to him: talking to the person next to him – me!

I am always mindful of God setting up opportunities for us to be an expressive embodiment of the divine, so as this young man turned to me and said hello, you could see in the back of his mind that what he wanted to say was, 'Well, all my technology has failed me, so I supposed I could talk to you!' I responded, as I generally do, with a smile and a hello with a gentle nod. We began to talk about normal surface things, but something seemed to be leading the atmosphere. It soon became apparent that he was having some serious issues with his father. We talked more deeply. I found myself giving illustrations from his technical concepts, of which I really know very little. But this young man seemed to be really getting it. We talked all the way to Berwick-upon-Tweed station, where I got off and he stayed on. As I left, he thanked me and told me that he was feeling much more at ease about life and his work and his relationship with his father.

I walked from the train and thought that was it, that was the encounter God has set up for me. But I was approached by a lady who had been able to hear all of what I had been saying to this young man. She asked me how it was that I was ready to engage in such a way when I was just on a train journey. I explained the whole concept which we are looking at today, and that actually I often had conversations like that. She was fascinated and asked, as she was a journalist, whether I would be happy to do an interview for local radio and newspaper about spirituality in the everyday and seeing the divine move through the normal things. I agreed, and we arranged a time to hold the interview in the prayer room of the Open

Gate retreat centre on Lindisfarne. Since that time, I have had some wonderful in-depth and insightful conversations with the journalist, and we are still friends. It seems that the conversation with the man on the train, whatever good that did him, was really about creating the environment for a more long-term conversational relationship to begin with someone else.

Contemplation

As we journey towards Easter, how do you understand journeys? Are they just a means to an end (literally sometimes)? Or are they a part of who you are and what you are doing? And are you mindful of the divine presence moving?

Reading

You were dead through the trespasses and sins in which you once lived, following the course of this world, following the ruler of the power of the air, the spirit that is now at work among those who are disobedient. All of us once lived among them in the passions of our flesh, following the desires of flesh and senses, and we were by nature children of wrath, like everyone else. But God, who is rich in mercy, out of the great love with which he loved us even when we were dead through our trespasses, made us alive together with Christ – by grace you have been saved – and raised us up with him and seated us with him in the heavenly places in Christ Jesus, so that in the ages to come he might show the immeasurable riches of his grace in kindness toward us in Christ Jesus. For by grace you have been saved through faith, and this is not your own doing; it is the gift of God – not the result of works, so that no one may boast. *For we are what he has made us, created in Christ Jesus for good works, which God prepared beforehand to be our way of life.*[55]

EPHESIANS 2:1–10

Prayer

Instigator of divine encounters, Creator of good works, cause me to develop the heart and mind always to be aware of your presence with me at all times and in all I do. May I be alert enough to discover the good works which you have set up for me to do. Amen

Tuesday

As the Celtic saints walked from one place to another, it is thought that they sang or chanted the psalms and spiritual songs. The journeys that they took every day, or on special occasions, were a part of the pilgrimage of life, and their awareness of the divine presence was enhanced by the deliberate focus of it through chanting or singing scripture, songs and especially the psalms.

When Aidan and his monks travelled from Iona to Northumbria, ending on Lindisfarne, the air of the journey would have been filled with the voices of the monks chanting the psalms. The sound would have reverberated around the countryside and risen up to heaven. It was, perhaps, a natural extension for the Celtic monks from this external practice that their inner journey, and their life journey, would have also been filled with the sound of psalms and spiritual songs. Or perhaps it was the other way around – perhaps the external expression was the natural result of the internal practice of filling their inner life journey with spiritual songs of praise. The journey itself was filled with praise: the external journey as well as the internal journey.

Music and song were a huge part of the Celtic and Anglo-Saxon culture, just like it is for ours today. Music and song seem to have been a deep aspect of who we are as people right from the start, just like story and poetry which we have already looked at.

Celtic music today usually has the flavour of pipes and whistles, perhaps even a harp, but is not likely to be much like the music that the Celtic saints heard or played a millennium and a half ago. Despite that, it is growing in popularity and there are some wonderful Christian bands who play this modern version of Celtic music. Included in these songs are those which are focused upon the crucifixion of Christ which can help us to connect more deeply with this story, this act from the past.[56]

We can have music wherever we go in our modern culture. iPods in our pockets, downloads on our phones – music really can be with us everywhere. But this is just the external sound. What about the internal sound which is playing on our life journey? What is the soundtrack that plays in your inner journey? Does this seep in from whatever music you listen to, or is the music you fill your world with an overflow of what is going on in your heart? And where does God fit into all of this?

Contemplation

As you go through your everyday life, what music sings from your soul? Does this music fill your surrounding world as well, or does the music from the outside penetrate your inner being? If so, what are you letting influence you? Is it life-giving? What songs could draw you more deeply along this particular path through Lent?

Reading

And let the peace of Christ rule in your hearts, to which indeed you were called in the one body. And be thankful. Let the word of Christ dwell in you richly; teach and admonish one another in all wisdom; and with gratitude in your hearts sing psalms, hymns, and spiritual songs to God. And whatever you do, in word or deed, do everything in the name of the Lord Jesus, giving thanks to God the Father through him.

COLOSSIANS 3:15–17

Prayer

God of music and song, God of the music of life, raise a song in my heart that will flow out into the life which I live. As I journey towards Easter through Lent, may my song reflect this wonderful, terrible, glorious act. Amen

Wednesday

Let me tell you one of the great legends of St Patrick. In 433, Patrick resolved to make a stand against the king for the gospel. It was one of the laws of the festival that the druids were then celebrating that, on what is Easter eve, the fires throughout the land should be extinguished in every hearth in Ireland. The death penalty awaited anyone who dared kindle their own fire before the first fire was lit by the High King's druid in Tara. When the king's fire was seen shining in the darkness of the night, all other fires could be lit, preferably by taking the fire from the main fire, symbolising the drawing into each home the spiritual belief of the druids. Yet Patrick, arriving at the hill of Slane in sight of the king's palace at Tara, lit an Easter fire before the High King's fire was lit.

King Laeghaire saw Patrick's fire, and asked who it was who had violated his law. The druids told him that if this fire were not put out before morning, it would never be extinguished in the land, and that the man who had lit it would be exalted above kings and princes. This was, of course, a metaphorical statement of a spiritual context, but of no little significance to the king's authority. Infuriated at these words, the king mounted his chariot and set out to meet the perpetrator, at the same time declaring his determination to put him to death. When Laeghaire came in sight of Patrick and his companions, he was warned by the druids not to go near the fire but to send for the man.

Patrick was not slow or fearful in answering the king's summons. As he drew near, he sang Psalm 20:7: 'Some take pride in chariots, and some in horses, but our pride is in the name of the Lord our God.' A contest of supernatural power followed in which Luchru, one of the druids, boasted that he had power to ascend to heaven. Then, in the sight of all, he rose up above the earth. In response, Patrick prayed, and his prayer brought the druid down, who lay lifeless on the earth. Seeing this, the king and his people became maddened and rose against Patrick to make an attempt on his life. But Patrick quoted from the psalms: 'Let God rise up, let his enemies be scattered; let those who hate him flee before him' (Psalm 68:1). God heard this prayer and sent a great wind that swept across the hillside, and in the dull light of the rising sun panic ensued, and the swords of the pagans were turned against each other. The queen, who was present, was won to the faith by this divine act. This victory ended the first day of Patrick's struggle at the hill of Slane near Tara.

King Laeghaire, amazed but still unconvinced, asked Patrick to come to see him at his palace when day had broken. The king determined to make another attempt to kill Patrick. With this purpose, he posted soldiers on all the roads that led from Slane to Tara. The soldiers of the king, who were lying in wait to slay Patrick and his company of seven monks, along with a young cleric, saw nothing except eight deer, including one fine stag at the front, followed by a fawn, which passed by on the path. And so Patrick and his companions, by divine intervention, avoided the trap of the king. On Easter Sunday, St Patrick arrived at Tara and appeared before the astonished king.

The longer-term result of these miraculous things was that Patrick was eventually given the freedom for his faith across Ireland.

Contemplation

This story from the life of Patrick shows an incredible belief in the power of the risen God. The work of the cross and resurrection was a work in which all power, in heaven and on earth, came under the subject of Christ and the breaking of sin and evil. How do you understand this power? How does it manifest in your life?

Reading

If then there is any encouragement in Christ, any consolation from love, any sharing in the Spirit, any compassion and sympathy, make my joy complete: be of the same mind, having the same love, being in full accord and of one mind. Do nothing from selfish ambition or conceit, but in humility regard others as better than yourselves. Let each of you look not to your own interests, but to the interests of others. Let the same mind be in you that was in Christ Jesus, who, though he was in the form of God, did not regard equality with God as something to be exploited, but emptied himself, taking the form of a slave, being born in human likeness. And being found in human form, he humbled himself and became obedient to the point of death – even death on a cross.

Therefore, God also highly exalted him and gave him the name that is above every name, so that at the name of Jesus every knee should bend, in heaven and on earth and under the earth, and every tongue should confess that Jesus Christ is Lord, to the glory of God the Father.

Therefore, my beloved, just as you have always obeyed me, not only in my presence, but much more now in my absence, work out your own salvation with fear and trembling; for it is God who is at work in you, enabling you both to will and to work for his good pleasure.

PHILIPPIANS 2:1–13

Prayer

Great and powerful God, as your power flows through the heavens and the earth, may it flow in and through me. May I, like Patrick, be willing to take a stand for the gospel as an active peacemaker. May I stand on the power in the name of Jesus. Amen

Thursday

Although for most of the Celtic saints, it seems clear that they saw themselves as part of the one universal (western) church, there were some significant differences in certain aspects of theology and ways of thinking about things like: how to be a Christian, the work of the cross, and the grace and mercy of the divine. One of those differences is how we view the core of who we are as humans, and what the work of the grace of God through the cross did.

For the Latin church, who had the teaching of original sin through Augustine of Hippo and others, the very core of the human being, their soul, was evil and fallen and required total transformation from one thing to another – a saved soul. For many Celtic Christians, there was a slightly different view. They believed that the very core of your being was the divine image, that each person was made in the divine image. Although this image had been tainted by sin and required the work of the cross of Christ, the very essence of our soul was therefore essentially good. This not only made a significant difference to how one saw other people, whether or not they were Christians, but it also made a difference to how one understood the work of the grace of God through the cross. This was one of the things which Augustine seemed to get confused about within the teachings of Pelagius.

In the book *Listening to the Heartbeat of God: A Celtic spirituality*, Philip Newell suggests:

> For Pelagius, evil was rather like an occupying army. The people yearn for liberation, but are bound by the forces of evil. Redemption, therefore, can be understood in terms of a setting free, a releasing of what we essentially are.[57]

This idea that we, or the souls of every human being, are like a community living in peace, but that has been occupied by an invading army (what sin has done), means that the work of the cross is a driving out of the sin which occupies our inner being, restoring us back to what we were originally – living in peace within ourselves in good relationship with our Maker.

Pelagius was, of course, using this illustration in a time and place where everyone knew exactly what it was to have an occupying army in control. Pelagius was, at this time, right at the heart of the Roman Empire. With this understanding, the work of the cross, the driving out of sin in us, could perhaps be seen as the never-ending work of becoming more like Christ, and is the 'releasing of what we essentially are' – perfect in righteousness – a perfect reflection of the divine image. As Pelagius himself suggests in his *Letter to Demetrias*, each individual *is* capable of living a holy and righteous life:

> Before the arrival of our Lord and Saviour some are reported to have lived holy and righteous lives; how much more possible must we believe that to be after the light of his coming, now that we have been instructed by the grace of Christ and reborn as better men: purified and cleansed by his blood, encouraged by his example to pursue perfect righteousness.[58]

If this is true, if sin is like an occupying army within us, and the work of the cross is the power to drive that occupying force out, what does that mean for us in our everyday life?

Contemplation

Have you ever thought of the effect of sin within you like that of an occupying army oppressing who you were created to be, stopping you reflecting properly the one in whose image you are made? Spend some time now thinking about what this means and how it might change the way you see others as well as yourself.

Reading

When one turns to the Lord, the veil is removed. Now the Lord is
the Spirit, and where the Spirit of the Lord is, there is freedom.
And all of us, with unveiled faces, seeing the glory of the Lord
as though reflected in a mirror, are being transformed into the
same image from one degree of glory to another; for this comes
from the Lord, the Spirit.

2 CORINTHIANS 3:16–18

Prayer

Holy and powerful one, drive out all that is within me which
is not of you. Come and bring freedom to my inner being,
and restore my soul to who I should be, who you originally
intended me to be. Amen

Friday

Yesterday, we looked at the thoughts of a Celtic saint from the fourth and fifth centuries. Today, we will look at similar thoughts from a ninth-century Celtic saint: John Scotus Eriugena. In his book *Journeys with Celtic Christians*, Rodney Newman suggests that for the Celtic Christians, 'salvation is not a matter of changing human beings into different people, from worthless to worthy. Salvation is the restoration, or a recovery, of the person God created us to be in the first place.'[59]

Yesterday, we saw that Pelagius suggested that evil was 'rather like an occupying army [where] the people yearn for liberation, but are bound by the forces of evil'.[60] A similar idea can be seen 400 years later in Eriugena's writing, where he states:

> Just as the skin of the human body is afflicted of the contagion and deformity of leprosy, so human nature was infected and corrupted by arrogant disobedience and made deformed and unlike its Creator. When it is freed from this leprosy by the medicine of divine grace, it will be restored to its original fairness of form.[61]

For Eriugena, then, the process of divine grace and the work of the cross of Christ was the working within each soul of a divine balm restoring a tainted 'skin'; the continuing transformation of the individual was a restoration of who the individual truly was. Just the same as Pelagius' thought, or the thought of Celtic Christians through the years, we are made in the divine image – we are 'fearfully and wonderfully made' (Psalm 139:14) – and the very core of who we are, the very essence of our being, is good, yet tainted by sin. The work of the cross is the divine heavenly balm which will restore our soul 'to its original fairness of form'.

For Eriugena, as for Pelagius, as for the Celtic saints in general, as it can be for us also – the grace and power of God through the work of the cross brings about a cleansing within us that means we can become who we were made to be in the first place, who we were made to be when God first knit us together in our mother's womb (Psalm 139:13).

Contemplation

In a similar contemplation to yesterday, have you ever thought of the effect of sin within you like that of a skin disease which is tainting you from who you were created to be, from reflecting properly the one in whose image you are made? Spend some time now thinking about what this means and how it might change the way you see others as well as yourself.

Reading

Once, when [Jesus] was in one of the cities, there was a man covered with leprosy. When he saw Jesus, he bowed with his face to the ground and begged him, 'Lord, if you choose, you can make me clean.' Then Jesus stretched out his hand, touched him, and said, 'I do choose. Be made clean.' Immediately the leprosy left him.

LUKE 5:12–13

Prayer

Healing Creator, cleanse me from my sin, clean me and make me as I was supposed to be. Draw me more and more into your likeness as you work on me in your grace with your divine balm. Amen

Saturday

This week, we have looked at the power of God and the power of the cross working in every part, and in the everyday life of each individual human being, including ourselves. We have seen what influence divine power can have on us and those around us if we allow it to flow through us and be a part of our everyday life.

Our own personal restoration, and that of every human being, back to what we were originally created to be, to be able to live out of the divine image within us, is something which we can gain through the work of the grace of God through the act of the cross of Christ.

God creates us. God with loving hands knits us together and moulds our being. God does not make mistakes. God does not make faulty goods. Somewhere along the line, this occupying army comes in, this skin disease creeps over our soul, but at the start of our own personal creation, when we begin, God's loving formation of our being creates the perfect human being – you – in the divine image.

As we journey through Lent and focus on this incredible and almighty act of Christ driving out the occupying army and cleansing us from the spiritual skin disease, we can begin to see the love with which we were made. We cannot go anywhere God is not, because God is everywhere, and he is setting up all sorts of opportunities for us to be able to live out this wonderful expression of divine love that is the grace and mercy of the cross.

As you pause today in our journey, take time to become aware of just how wonderful you are; just how special you are; just how much care and love God put into creating you to be you – untainted, unoccupied – the perfect you that you could be, just as God intended. This is the you which you can be because of the work of the cross. You, being perfectly you!

Contemplation

Who am I? Who am I supposed to be? Who am I without the occupying army of sin, without the skin disease of sin? What part can I play in the restoration process?

Reading

O Lord, you have searched me and known me.
You know when I sit down and when I rise up;
    you discern my thoughts from far away.
You search out my path and my lying down,
    and are acquainted with all my ways.
Even before a word is on my tongue,
    O Lord, you know it completely.
You hem me in, behind and before,
    and lay your hand upon me.
Such knowledge is too wonderful for me;
    it is so high that I cannot attain it.

Where can I go from your spirit?
    Or where can I flee from your presence?
If I ascend to heaven, you are there;
    if I make my bed in Sheol, you are there.
If I take the wings of the morning
    and settle at the farthest limits of the sea,
even there your hand shall lead me,
    and your right hand shall hold me fast.
If I say, 'Surely the darkness shall cover me,
    and the light around me become night,'

even the darkness is not dark to you;
  the night is as bright as the day,
  for darkness is as light to you.

For it was you who formed my inward parts;
  you knit me together in my mother's womb.
I praise you, for I am fearfully and wonderfully made.
  Wonderful are your works;
that I know very well.
  My frame was not hidden from you,
when I was being made in secret,
  intricately woven in the depths of the earth.
Your eyes beheld my unformed substance.
In your book were written
  all the days that were formed for me,
  when none of them as yet existed.
How weighty to me are your thoughts, O God!
  How vast is the sum of them!
I try to count them – they are more than the sand;
  I come to the end – I am still with you.

PSALM 139:1–18

Prayer

Almighty Creator, intimate friend, loving Father, restorer of all that I am, I pledge to work with you to restore the beautiful being which you created, beginning with the declaration that I am wonderful! I say this not because of ego, but because the scripture says that you made me, I am one of your works and that your works are wonderful. Thank you. May my restoration begin with my belief in myself. Amen

Contemplation
for the fifth **Sunday** in Lent

How do you understand the power of the cross and
the restoration of the divine image within yourself?
What more could you do to strengthen this belief?

Week five

Monday

One of the most complete liturgical manuscripts we have from the historic Celtic church is known as the Stowe Missal.[62] This was written in the monastic centre in Tallaght (now a suburb of Dublin) at the end of the eighth century. It is known as the Stowe Missal as it was once part of the *Stowe Manuscripts*, a collection of around 2,000 Irish and Anglo-Saxon manuscripts which were kept by the first Marquess of Buckingham and his son the first Duke of Buckingham, at Stowe House near Buckingham in the early 19th century. Almost all of this collection is now in either the British Library in London or the Royal Irish Academy in Dublin.

The Stowe Missal is around 60 leaves of illuminated writing explaining the order of the Eucharist service of the monastic centre, along with some prayers and hymns.

This week we will be looking at the Stowe Missal, unpacking the Celtic journey through the Mass of the Holy Eucharist.

The first thing we need to understand as we gaze at this ancient sacrament is the Celtic approach to liturgy. Today, liturgy is often seen simply as written words which we say to lead us through a service, but liturgy has a much greater, more mystical depth to it than that. Liturgy is:

> … a dynamic encounter crossing several thresholds. It is on earth, but that place on earth is also part of heaven… For the people for whom [the Stowe Missal] was produced the liturgy was something greater than them[selves]… Their task was to enter into it and be absorbed within it… Each act of liturgy was

a chance to re-enter and be absorbed more completely into this whole Christ [experience].[63]

No liturgy is more able to do this, to absorb us more completely into the Christ experience, than eucharistic liturgy. So the Stowe Missal gives us a chance to discover the Celtic journey into this deep mystical encounter with Christ at the Lord's table.

The liturgy within the Stowe Missal is rich with meaning and metaphor. Every act is written out and explained so that the priests and the congregation knew exactly what was going on and what it all meant. Specific chants and hymns went into certain sections of the service, each reflecting what was being enacted by the priests. This all aided the people to engage more deeply and be absorbed more completely into the divine presence being drawn down into the physical place in which they were celebrating this act.

What the Stowe Missal shows us is that the Eucharist, for the Celtic Christians, was not just a service which they did because they felt they should, or even because they wanted to. It was a sacred mystical act which drew them closer to God and enabled them truly to imagine what it would have been like for Christ on the cross.

Every Eucharist was a mystical thanksgiving with deep symbolic meaning.

Contemplation

How do you view liturgy? Is it just the words which guide us through the service, or is there something more to it? What about the Eucharist, or Communion itself? Is every Eucharist a mystical thanksgiving with deep symbolic meaning for you? If not, why not?

Reading

Then came the day of Unleavened Bread, on which the Passover lamb had to be sacrificed. So Jesus sent Peter and John, saying, 'Go and prepare the Passover meal for us that we may eat it.' They asked him, 'Where do you want us to make preparations for it?' 'Listen,' he said to them, 'when you have entered the city, a man carrying a jar of water will meet you; follow him into the house he enters and say to the owner of the house, 'The teacher asks you, "Where is the guest room, where I may eat the Passover with my disciples?"' He will show you a large room upstairs, already furnished. Make preparations for us there.' So they went and found everything as he had told them; and they prepared the Passover meal.

When the hour came, he took his place at the table, and the apostles with him. He said to them, 'I have eagerly desired to eat this Passover with you before I suffer; for I tell you, I will not eat it until it is fulfilled in the kingdom of God.'

LUKE 22:7–16

Prayer

Holy one, as I see and read the words of liturgy, may I see beyond the written words to the deeper meanings behind it, especially when it comes to the Eucharist. May every Eucharist be for me a mystical thanksgiving with deep symbolic meaning. Amen

Tuesday

Numbers, to the Celtic people just like to the Jewish people, were important and symbolic. You find that in Celtic spirituality, the number three appears as a sacred number, just like it does in Jewish spirituality. Celtic Triads – such as these from around the same time as the Stowe Missal: 'Three candles that illumine every darkness: truth, nature, knowledge'; 'These three have the lightest hearts: a student reading his psalms, a young lad who has left off his boyhood clothes for good, a maid who has been made a woman'[64] – are meant as snippets of wisdom, proverbs to help the reader or hearer in their everyday life. The significance here is not only the words, but the fact that they come as triads, in sets of three.

Reflecting this aspect of the culture and spiritual belief, the number three also appears in the Stowe Missal, and so therefore we can assume in other Celtic eucharistic liturgy and services. *The Tract on the Mass in the Stowe Missal* is a list of 19 things guiding the leader through the eucharistic Mass. Numbers eight and nine on the list are where the appearance of the number three comes, once in each:

> When 'Jesus took the bread' is sung, the priest bows three times to repent of his sins. He offers the chalice to God and chants 'God, have mercy on me.' The people kneel and no one speaks in case it should disturb the priest, for it is right that his mind does not turn from God while he chants this lesson. Hence it is called the 'dangerous address'.[65]

But why does the priest bow three times for his sins? Why specifically three and not more or less? This is answered in the next section when the priest literally takes steps for the sake of the people.

The three steps backwards which the priest takes and the three steps forward is the triad in which everyone sins, that is, in word, thought, and deed, and this is the triad whereby we are renewed again and move toward Christ's body.[66]

So the three bows and the three steps back and forth represent the three ways in which we all sin, in our words, in our thoughts, and in our deeds. (Did you notice that there are also three acts: bowing, stepping backward and stepping forward?) These three aspects to our lives cover all that we are. Our words, in the modern context, are not just those which are spoken, but those which we type out on to social media or in emails. It seems that so many people type things out and click 'send' without reading through what they have written. These days, the words we 'speak' flow so freely that we do not even give ourselves the chance to think about them. This is obviously also true for the words we speak verbally. Our thoughts are always a nuisance; they are the things which we perhaps struggle with the most. If we are aware of ourselves, then we can temper our words and our actions, but our thoughts? They are a different matter, a harder beast to tame. It *is* possible to do this. I, along with many others through the years, have written on Christian meditation[67] and the practices and principles of settling one's thoughts down and being able to 'take every thought captive' (2 Corinthians 10:5).

However, we all need to seek forgiveness for our words, thoughts and deeds and, as the Stowe Missal says, in our repentance we are also 'renewed again and move toward Christ's body'.

Contemplation

Think upon the three ways in which we each fail God – in word, thought, and deed. Taking each one in turn, in what ways have you failed God recently?

Reading

Forgive us our debts,
    as we also have forgiven our debtors.
And do not bring us to the time of trial,
    but rescue us from the evil one.
For if you forgive others their trespasses, your heavenly Father
will also forgive you; but if you do not forgive others, neither
will your Father forgive your trespasses.

MATTHEW 6:12–15

Prayer

**Gracious and loving one, forgive me for my shortcomings,
forgive me for how I have failed in word, and in thought, and
in deed. I bring before you now these things...** *[add your own
personal repentance here].* **Thank you for your forgiveness,
and may I live a life expressing that forgiveness to others.
Amen**

Wednesday

We know, both from the size of the Eucharist plates which have been found from this period, and from the way in which it is described in the liturgies, that the Celtic Christians used a full loaf for the bread in Communion, and broke it as part of the ceremony. The Stowe Missal tells us that there were various symbolic aspects of breaking the bread. For example, have you ever been leading a Eucharist service with a full loaf and struggled to break it? Most of us simply try to pretend it isn't happening and try to make it look as effortless as possible. But for the Celtic Christians, it seems, this was all part of the symbolism: 'The effort [the priest] makes to break [the bread] represents the insults and the beating and the seizing of Christ.'[68]

Once the bread was broken in two to represent the broken body of Christ on the cross, it was then held back together again by the priest to represent the wholeness of Christ's body after the resurrection. However, this was not the end of the breaking of the bread. It wasn't left to have a small piece broken off when giving it out to the people, or left for people to tear a piece off as it was given to them, but the priest broke the full loaf up and arranged it on the plate in the shape of a cross in pieces. The Stowe Missal describes ways in which the broken bread was arranged in different forms of the cross for different services.[69] I particularly like the arrangement of the broken bread for the eucharistic Mass at the celebration feasts of Easter, Christmas and Pentecost. This takes the form of a fully created equal-armed Celtic cross which was carefully broken into 65 parts and looked something like this:[70]

Each section was for a specific set of people: the central piece was for the celebrant of the Mass, symbolising the secrets kept in the heart. The upper part of the shaft of the cross was for the bishops; the left portion of the crosspiece for priests; the right portion of the crosspiece for those lower than priest; the lower portion of the stem was for monks and penitents; the upper left quadrant of the circle was for young clerics; the upper right quadrant for children; the lower left was for those who are truly repentant; the lower right was for those who were married and those who have never before received Communion. The body of Christ was therefore shared out equally and specifically to those who were present.

Once the piece was given to each person, there were also guidelines on how to eat it. One of these was the instruction that 'it is not right to swallow the piece without tasting it, as it is improper not to seek to introduce savours into the mysteries of God',[71] bringing in the Celtic holistic theology that the body and physical sensations, such as taste, were all a part of our connection and relationship with God; they did not believe in the dualism of separating physical and spiritual.

This very carefully organised and executed breaking, distributing and eating of the bread (and there is a great deal more which I have left out) shows just how special and sacred the Celtic Christians viewed this service.

Tomorrow, we look at the cup of wine.

Contemplation

The bread in the Eucharist is a representation of the body of Christ. Contemplate the biblical concept of the bread in the Eucharist, and how it is described above.

Reading

Then he took a loaf of bread, and when he had given thanks, he broke it and gave it to them, saying, 'This is my body, which is given for you. Do this in remembrance of me.'
LUKE 22:19

Prayer

Broken Saviour, tortured, flayed, pierced and nailed, ridiculed, arms outstretched, in wretched pain, those who loved you watched in vain, their hearts breaking, as you were lain on the tree… All this for me, all this to set me free, free from my sin, broken for me, so undeserved. I want to thank you Lord, I long to serve, I kneel before your Majesty.[72]

Thursday

The single chalice used by the Celtic Christians in the eucharistic Mass was a good-sized cup, like a large quaich with handles. Those which have been found from the period of time that the Stowe Missal comes, such as that found in the Derrynaflan Hoard, are large enough to hold (without filling it too close to the brim) around one and a half modern bottles of wine.[73] The Stowe Missal also describes dunking the entire loaf of bread into the chalice: 'The submerging of the two halves [of the bread] in the chalice represents the submersion of Christ's body in his blood after his wounding on the cross.'[74] This was enough wine for each person in a group of around 60–70 to have a good-sized mouthful, and it seems that they weren't shy in taking it either – no gentle sips as we are perhaps used to today. Within the Rule of Columbanus, for example, we find written a sanction for 'him who has bitten the cup of salvation with his teeth'![75] This perhaps goes back to the final aspect that we looked at yesterday in the taking of the bread, about ensuring you get a good sense of flavour and taste as part of the holistic sacred experience. No tiny individual glasses or gentle lip-wetting for the Celtic Christians when it comes to drinking the wine in the Eucharist.

The Stowe Missal describes the pouring of water into the chalice first before the wine to represent the people in the church, then wine is added later. The wine therefore represents Christ's divinity mixed with his humanity and his coming to be one with the people of earth through the incarnation.

We also find in the Stowe Missal that, when the chalice had been taken by each person and handed back to the priest, the priest would then circle the head of each person with the chalice in a Caim prayer before moving on to the next person. A Caim prayer is a prayer of encircling protection that was used by the Celtic Christians: the asking of either divine or angelic protection to surround the person, or whatever it was that was being encircled. Ninian of Whithorn in the fourth century famously encircled a herd of cows in a famer's field with a Caim prayer, protecting them from marauders and rustlers. Within the Eucharist, this, in my understanding, is a prayer for each person to be covered in the protective blood of Christ. The power which is in the blood of Christ was seen and expressed in Celtic Christianity.

This act with the bread and wine in the Eucharist was more than just a remembering for the Celtic Christians, as we might see it and present it today; it was a reimmersing of one's self in the blood of Christ as part of the holistic understanding they had of life, and a 'chance to re-enter and be absorbed more completely into this whole Christ [experience]'.[76]

Contemplation

The blood of Christ shed on the cross has power: power to purify us from all sin (1 John 1:7), to draw us near to God (Ephesians 2:13) and to cleanse us from all that separates us from God (Hebrews 9:13–14). How do you understand the power of the blood of Christ? If it can do these things, what can that lead us to?

Reading

> After supper he took another cup of wine and said, 'This cup is the new covenant between God and his people – an agreement confirmed with my blood, which is poured out as a sacrifice for you.'
> LUKE 22:20 (NLT)

Caim prayer

Encircle me, Lord, keep harm without, keep safety within;
Encircle me, Lord, keep turmoil without, keep peace within;
Encircle me, Lord, keep evil out, keep your goodness in.

Friday

During the distribution of the bread and wine in most churches today, there is usually either a song sung or some music played. According to the Stowe Missal, the Celtic Eucharist services were no different. What is called 'Chant 2 (Pacem meam)' is to be chanted during the distribution of Communion.[77]

This interactive chant with leaders' parts and responses, as well as full psalms, was written to a length which would be roughly equal to the time it would take for the 60–70 people to take Communion. This gives us some idea of how the Celtic Christians understood this service, taking time with the chunk of bread they took and savouring it, and taking a good mouthful of wine ('drinking' in remembrance rather than just sipping), then having a Caim prayer prayed over you one person at a time.

The chant to be used during the distribution of the bread and wine begins with verses of scripture and statements about God's peace being given to us. This is a wonderful way to begin the act of deeply engaging in the Christ experience, by being reminded of the divine peace which we can possess because of the act of the cross and resurrection of Christ. This first stanza then ends (after having recited Psalm 23 in the middle of it) with John 6:56, reminding us that anyone who eats the bread and drinks the wine remains in Christ, and Christ remains in them; the abiding divine presence which brings peace dwells within us and we dwell within it. This is the first thought in the Communion hymn/chant.

Psalms 24 and 25 are then recited in full, punctuated between with John 6:50–51:

This is the bread that comes down from heaven, so that one may eat of it and not die. I am the living bread that came down from heaven. Whoever eats of this bread will live forever; and the bread that I will give for the life of the world is my flesh.

Shortly after this, Psalm 43, which is entitled 'Defend me, O God' in the Missal, is recited. This is, perhaps, a reinforcement of the Caim prayers being said with the chalice circling the people's heads.

[Defend] me, O God, and defend my cause
     against an ungodly people;
from those who are deceitful and unjust
     deliver me!
For you are the God in whom I take refuge…
O send out your light and your truth;
     let them lead me…
Why are you cast down, O my soul,
     and why are you disquieted within me?
Hope in God; for I shall again praise him,
     my help and my God.

PSALM 43 (abridged)

A reminder that the Eucharist was a thanksgiving feast is given with the words, 'This is the sacred body of our Lord [Alleluia]; the blood of our Saviour, Alleluia; feast, all of you, on it for eternal life. Alleluia.'[78]

Finally, the Communion hymn/chant ends with a long stanza of praise and repentance.

This hymn, which was sung or chanted during the distribution of the bread and wine, holds all the elements which are essential to the act itself: the bringing of divine peace to us; the dwelling of Christ within us and us within Christ; the protection we have as we live 'hidden with Christ in God' (Colossians 3:3); and the praise we can bring because of our repentance and God's forgiveness.

The cross was a symbol of divine peace and God's power, drawing us into the divine presence.

Contemplation

Spend time with God dwelling on the focal points of this eucharistic hymn:

Divine peace to us; the dwelling of Christ within us and us within Christ; the protection we have; and the praise we bring because of our repentance and God's forgiveness.

Reading

'I am the living bread that came down from heaven. Anyone who eats this bread will live forever; and this bread, which I will offer so the world may live, is my flesh.'

Then the people began arguing with each other about what he meant. 'How can this man give us his flesh to eat?' they asked.

So Jesus said again, 'I tell you the truth, unless you eat the flesh of the Son of Man and drink his blood, you cannot have eternal life within you. But anyone who eats my flesh and drinks my blood has eternal life, and I will raise that person at the last day. For my flesh is true food, and my blood is true drink. Anyone who eats my flesh and drinks my blood remains in me, and I in him. I live because of the living Father who sent me; in the same way, anyone who feeds on me will live because of me. I am the true bread that came down from heaven. Anyone who eats this bread will not die as your ancestors did (even though they ate the manna) but will live forever.'

JOHN 6:51–58 (NLT)

Prayer

Almighty Saviour, as I dwell with you, you dwell with me; as I contemplate the act of the Eucharist, draw me closer to you and guard my heart and mind with your peace. Amen

Saturday

The cross of Christ is the very centre, the very focus of the period of Lent. Like a runner with their eyes fixed on the finish line, during Lent our eyes are fixed upon the cross of Christ. Although we cannot forget the grand victory of the resurrection, the work of the cross was the start and so, in our lead-up to the Easter weekend, and at every Eucharist, our eyes are fixed upon the cross.

For Celtic Christians, the cross was a deeply powerful symbol. One of the most famous modern symbols of Celtic culture is the cross, found on jewellery, book covers, tattoos and album covers, as well as many other places. Typically, the Celtic cross has a circle around it, which has numerous and different explanations, which we don't have opportunity to go into here, but the cross itself is there at the centre of Celtic Christianity.

The Celtic Christians believed that the cross held great power, and could be used a bit like a weapon in spiritual warfare. One of the reasons for this was because the main teaching of the cross of Christ in the time of the Celtic church wasn't the substitution atonement theology, which is the main teaching of the cross today (that Jesus died in my place so I could be made right with God), but which has only been the main teaching in Christianity for the past 800 to 900 years. The main teaching of the work of the cross for the first thousand years or so of the Christian faith, at least in the Celtic and Anglo-Saxon nations, as far as we understand, was the *Christus Victor* teaching: that is, that Christ died on the cross to defeat all the works of evil and to defeat Satan. Such verses as Colossians 2:15, which says, 'In this way, he disarmed the spiritual rulers and authorities. He shamed them publicly by his victory over them on the cross' (NLT), and 1 John 3:8, which says, 'The Son of God was revealed for this purpose, to destroy the works of the devil', were the keystones to this theology.

In *Water from an Ancient Well*, Kenneth McIntosh tells us this:

> On the cross Christ stepped into the human arena where we all confront death and the other works of Satan. Like the bravest of knights, he fought with these terrifying enemies and was victorious; he forced them to release humanity from their grip.[79]

From this understanding, within the culture of the warrior saga and song of the Celts and Anglo-Saxons, a poem/song of the cross of Christ arose known as *The Dream of the Rood* ('rood' being an old English word for 'cross'). During Holy Week, we will look more deeply into that epic warrior poem of Christ on the cross defeating evil in the spiritual battle.

This belief in the power of the cross of Christ meant that prayers also arose which invoked that power to aid and protect the people as they went about their business and daily lives, as well as the monks and nuns on mission, as this verse from a prayer in the *Carmina Gadelica*[80] shows:

> Be the cross of Christ between me and the fays [evil spirits]
> That move occultly out and in
> Be the cross of Christ between me and all ill,
> All ill-will, and ill-mishap.[81]

The cross of Christ, for the Celtic Christians, had power over evil; the work of Christ on the cross has defeated the power of Satan and all evil spirits, and so therefore it could bring protection over the power of evil if the power of the cross was invoked.

Contemplation

How do you view the cross of Christ? How do you understand the work of the cross? Does this understanding shown here, the *Christus Victor* model, bring a new and fresh perspective to the work of Christ on the cross? Have you ever used the power of the cross for protection? Might you?

Reading

> For Christ did not send me to baptise but to proclaim the gospel, and not with eloquent wisdom, so that the cross of Christ might not be emptied of its power.
> For the message about the cross is foolishness to those who are perishing, but to us who are being saved it is the power of God.
> 1 CORINTHIANS 1:17–18

Also read again Colossians 2:15 and 1 John 3:8.

Prayer

> **Christ who died on the cross to defeat the power of evil and all the works of Satan, I ask that you cause the power of the cross to come and surround and protect me now. As all negative spiritual forces may look upon me, may they see the power of the cross of Christ before me. May the power of the cross, this work to defeat the power of evil, stay with me today. Amen**

Contemplation
for Palm Sunday

Contemplate the coming victory and triumphal
entry by reading John 12:12–19.

Holy Week

Holy Week
Monday

When we looked at the poems and hymns and hero sagas of the Celtic Christians earlier in our Lenten journey, I briefly mentioned *The Dream of the Rood*.[82] This week, we will spend a few days looking more into that epic saga telling the story of the passion of Christ. *The Dream of the Rood* is the story of Christ's death set firmly within the hero saga style with the theology of *Christus Victor* squarely at the centre.

The most complete version of this Christocentric hero saga is the *Vercelli Text*, a manuscript of Old English poetry dating from the tenth century. However, sections of the text can be found engraved in runes in the dialect of the Northumbrian Angles around the edges of a large stone cross known as the Ruthwell Cross. This cross is dated somewhere between the late seventh and early ninth century, so let's say somewhere within the eighth century. This is the same sort of time that Bede was living and writing. For such a thing to be carved into a stone cross, it is most likely that the poem had been around in the oral tradition of the storytellers for quite some time before. So, we can fairly confidently assume that this hero saga of Christ on the cross known as *The Dream of the Rood* was around during the 'Celtic Christian' era of Northumbrian Britain.

The poem is a man's dream of the actual cross of Christ telling the story of the crucifixion. He dreams of the cross as both blood-drenched gallows and a glowing jewel-encrusted projection of glory.

In this poem, Christ is no sacrificial victim, as he is often portrayed in modern stories and films, but he is a hero, a warrior king coming to the battleground of the cross, and he is a *Dryhtnes*. This last word translates from the Old English as 'Lord', not unusual you might think, but, according to Robert Boenig in *Anglo-Saxon Spirituality*, the word *Dryhtnes* was 'originally the designation of a warlord in charge of a band of warriors'.[83] In short, the Christ presented here in this poem is someone with whom the Celtic and Anglo-Saxon warrior culture could identify. Although the battle is firmly set within the spiritual realm and is in no way promoting physical violence, the way in which Christ is referred to in it would be very easy for the ancient culture to identify with.

When the Rood speaks to the dreaming man, for example, about becoming the jewel-encrusted projection of glory after the crucifixion is over, it speaks in a way akin to a faithful Anglo-Saxon warrior being rewarded by their *Dryhtnes* after victory in battle. The dreamer himself then replies in a typical Anglo-Saxon way, which would suggest that he too would like to follow the *Dryhtnes* of this rewarded hero, the Rood.

As we unpack this poem a little during this week, remember that scripture tells us that there is a battle, but that Christ has won the victory. Even if you haven't thought of it this way before, even if you struggle to see it this way now, try to approach this poem of an event which will be all too familiar to you with different eyes, with Celtic/Anglo-Saxon eyes, with eyes as if you were from the eighth-century culture of the British Isles.

So pay attention and listen, as we hear the loveliest of dreams, that which was dreamt in the darkness of night while all those of sensible minds slept...[84]

Contemplation

Have you ever thought of viewing the cross and the act of Christ coming and dying on the cross as a battle scene? How often do you view the Christian life as a battle?

Reading

Finally, be strong in the Lord and in the strength of his power. Put on the whole armour of God, so that you may be able to stand against the wiles of the devil. For our struggle is not against enemies of blood and flesh, but against the rulers, against the authorities, against the cosmic powers of this present darkness, against the spiritual forces of evil in the heavenly places. Therefore, take up the whole armour of God, so that you may be able to withstand on that evil day, and having done everything, to stand firm. Stand therefore, and fasten the belt of truth around your waist, and put on the breastplate of righteousness. As shoes for your feet put on whatever will make you ready to proclaim the gospel of peace. With all of these, take the shield of faith, with which you will be able to quench all the flaming arrows of the evil one. Take the helmet of salvation, and the sword of the Spirit, which is the word of God.

Pray in the Spirit at all times in every prayer and supplication. To that end keep alert and always persevere in supplication for all the saints.

EPHESIANS 6:10–18

Prayer

Great and mighty God, conquering hero, as the Easter weekend approaches, I ask that you reveal to me the meaning of the cross as a battleground, that I would pledge my allegiance again to you, my *Dryhtnes*, my Lord and King, ready to stand for you in the spiritual battle. Amen

Holy Week
Tuesday

For today's focus, as we look at this epic hero saga, we are going to look at how it depicts Christ's approach to the cross. We are used to seeing a beaten and bloody Christ falling and stumbling along a road, carrying a heavy beam or cross to his execution place, weakened by the flogging which he had received. This pulls on modern heartstrings and on our mindset of being historically and literally accurate about things to give them their full effect, a modern belief that only the factually accurate presentation is useful for understanding the things which happened. But this is not how it worked all those years ago. For the Celtic and Anglo-Saxon culture, the inspiration of the story was of greater importance than factual accuracy. Imagery and metaphor were the important things. So, in *The Dream of the Rood*, we do not see a weakened and stumbling Jesus; instead, we are introduced to 'the young hero' who was hurrying 'with great eagerness to climb on [the cross]… He ascended the wretched gallows… when he wanted to redeem mankind.'[85]

This depiction of Christ as a young hero bravely striding towards the battleground (what the cross is depicted as) sets our eyes firmly within the spiritual realms rather than the physical, which is exactly what this saga is all about: the spiritual battle of the work of the cross rather than the physical reality of what happened historically. In this way, we are drawn into metaphorical and allegorical scenes which describe the spiritual effect of the cross.

The Rood describes how it trembled as Christ, the hero, made physical contact with it: 'I quivered when the hero clasped me,' one translation says.[86] Another says, 'I trembled when the hero hugged me.'[87] This reaction of the cross at the touch of its Creator is wonderfully telling of the power believed to be in this act. The Rood goes on to say that it took some doing to stay standing at this point, but that is exactly what it did as this was the powerful and mighty King – Christ – who it could not dishonour by falling.

What we have in the first part of this poem is a vision of Christ as he may have been in his spirit, rather than his body. Having drawn his resolve together in the garden of Gethsemane, he came to the cross physically weakened by the ordeal he had been through, but spiritually strong, knowing what this meant to all people and all things in both directions of linear history.

Christ is depicted here as ready for battle, eager to make the choice to go into this fight which would redeem humanity and reconcile all things back to the Creator. We are introduced to the brave hero King staring death in the face without a flinching heart.

Contemplation

Spend time thinking upon the idea of Christ approaching the cross in eagerness, wanting to save humanity and restore all things back to the Creator. See him as a brave hero 'hugging' or 'clasping' the cross in order to begin the battle which he knows he will win.

Reading

Then the soldiers led him into the courtyard of the palace (that is, the governor's headquarters); and they called together the whole cohort. And they clothed him in a purple cloak; and after twisting some thorns into a crown, they put it on him. And they began saluting him, 'Hail, King of the Jews!' They struck his head with a reed, spat upon him, and knelt down in homage to him. After mocking him, they stripped him of the purple cloak and put his own clothes on him. Then they led him out to crucify him.

They compelled a passer-by, who was coming in from the country, to carry his cross; it was Simon of Cyrene, the father of Alexander and Rufus. Then they brought Jesus to the place called Golgotha (which means the place of a skull). And they offered him wine mixed with myrrh; but he did not take it.

MARK 15:16–23

Prayer

King of the universe, Lord of all things, thank you that you went to the cross for me, but also to save everything from the clasp of sin. Thank you that you approached this knowing the joy set before you (Hebrews 12:2), and went with an eager heart, though weak in body. Raise my spirit to step into the trials I face with that same heart. Amen

Holy Week
Wednesday

We will come back to Christ on the cross on Friday. For the next couple of days, we will jump ahead of ourselves a little to be able to look at more of this saga. Today, we will look at the removal of Christ's body from the cross, and tomorrow we will look at the ending stanzas.

In three of the gospel accounts of Jesus being taken from the cross, Joseph of Arimathea is the only one named to have taken the body of Jesus down, wrapped him and taken him to a tomb. John's gospel tells us that Nicodemus, whose visit to Jesus is recorded in John 3, also came and helped Joseph. The reality is that it would have taken more than one or two men to do this job, despite the fact that only one or two are named in the Bible.

In *The Dream of the Rood*, we are told that numerous people came to help with this. This act was done by 'troops'[88] of 'warriors'[89] who had come from afar, eager to help the prince after battle, to be there for their fallen hero, where they 'laid down the limb-weary one' and 'stood about his head';[90] 'they beheld there the Lord of heaven; and there he rested a while, worn out after battle'.[91]

We see here in this section of the epic saga how the concept of the spiritual battle is still at the forefront of the narrative, even at the removal of the body of Christ from the cross. Christ is now worn out after the great battle he has fought on the cross. Evil is vanquished but Christ, the warrior king, is exhausted. But notice also that the followers of Christ are now called 'warriors'. We are all in this battle. Christ is the great warrior king who went alone into the battle on the cross, but those who follow this *Dryhtnes* are also warriors in the spiritual battle.

After taking the body of Christ from the cross, this troop of warriors created a grave in which to lay their fallen king, and they sang a lament, a woeful dirge at eventide. This is, of course, reminiscent of how the Celtic and Anglo-Saxon warriors acted. The songs of the fallen were sung in the mead halls in the evenings. The glorious battles and the valour shown by the great warriors and warrior kings were remembered in lamenting song. We see here, once again, the expression of the story reaching into the culture in ways which made sense to it, which those from it would understand.

Then, after the lament was sung, these troops left the body of the King in the grave and the body lay alone and grew cold. The Rood stayed standing, overlooking the now quiet grave until it was taken down and buried in the ground.

Contemplation

Where do you see yourself in this eternal epic saga? On Monday, we looked at the scripture which makes the boldest statement about the spiritual battle we are in. Do you see yourself as a spiritual warrior? Remembering the difference between the common modern physical depiction of Christ approaching and on the cross, compared to the Celtic/Anglo-Saxon depiction, seeing things from a spiritual perspective, do you see yourself as a warrior? What would it mean in a spiritual context if you did?

Reading

After these things, Joseph of Arimathea, who was a disciple of Jesus, though a secret one because of his fear of the Jews, asked Pilate to let him take away the body of Jesus. Pilate gave him permission; so he came and removed his body. Nicodemus, who had at first come to Jesus by night, also came, bringing a mixture of myrrh and aloes, weighing about a hundred pounds. They took the body of Jesus and wrapped it with the spices in linen cloths, according to the burial custom of the Jews. Now there was a garden in the place where he was crucified, and in the garden there was a new tomb in which no one had ever been laid. And so, because it was the Jewish day of Preparation, and the tomb was nearby, they laid Jesus there.

JOHN 19:38–42

Prayer

Dryhtnes, as the warriors Joseph and Nicodemus took your body from the cross and lay it in the grave, in that same dedication I give my life to you in the spiritual battle. Under the covering of the protection of your victory and your kingship over all things, call me to arms that I would fight all that wars against your kingdom on this earth. Amen

Maundy Thursday

As this epic story of the crucifixion draws to a close, the Rood makes a request to the dreamer: 'Now I beseech you, my beloved hero, that you proclaim this dream to the people.'[92] The dreamer is asked to pass on this story to those who will listen, just like Cædmon with his dreams. It is in passing on these great divine dreams that the glory of the story of God and the works done through Christ are placed into the hearts of all who have ears to hear. The inspiration of Cædmon's Bible stories, and the influence of this epic hero saga of the work of the cross, was what would draw many to Christianity in that day.

In this section of the poem, we also find another link with Cædmon: a term which we have already come across in a previous poem on our Lenten journey, a term that the Celtic/Anglo-Saxons used in poems and song for the world in which we live. This term that Cædmon used in the seventh century, and which J.R.R. Tolkien used in the 20th, is of course 'this middle-earth'[93] to which Christ will return at the end of time to judge all things and all people. We have in the few lines here surrounding 'middle earth' a statement which we are likely all familiar with, although worded differently to reflect the flow of the whole poem; we have the statement that Christ died, that Christ is risen, that Christ ascended into heaven and that Christ will come again to judge the living and the dead. The Rood's final words to the dreamer, flowing off this thought, are that no one who has turned to Christ need be afraid at the end when Christ returns as judge, but that 'through that cross each soul shall seek a kingdom away from the world's ways, he who wishes to dwell with the Wielder'.[94]

The final flourish to the end of the poem is then the dreamer speaking about his time here on earth. It seems that he has lost many friends – 'they have journeyed on from the joys of this world to find the King of Glory, they live in heaven with the High Father, dwell in splendour'[95] – and he desires to be with them. But the final lines are those of a wondrous return of a conquering hero. We end with Christ returning into heaven after his ascension: 'When He, Almighty Ruler, returned with a thronging host of spirits to God's kingdom, to joy amongst the angels… then their King, Almighty God, entered His own country.'[96] Christ, the conquering hero, returns to his home to sit as reigning king eternally!

Contemplation

The telling of this tale at the time it was written or in oral tradition was a way in which the Christians connected with the people and the culture. How might we tell this same story today to make it relevant so that people are drawn to it like it was something new, not something old from a different time which they cannot connect with? Ask God to give you new ways of telling this epic tale of the victorious battle against evil, the saving of humanity and creation, and reuniting all things with God.

Reading

And I heard a loud voice from the throne saying, 'See, the home of God is among mortals. He will dwell with them; they will be his peoples, and God himself will be with them; he will wipe every tear from their eyes. Death will be no more; mourning and crying and pain will be no more, for the first things have passed away.'

And the one who was seated on the throne said, 'See, I am making all things new.' Also he said, 'Write this, for these words are trustworthy and true.' Then he said to me, 'It is done! I am the Alpha and the Omega, the beginning and the end. To the thirsty I will give water as a gift from the spring of the water of life. Those who conquer will inherit these things, and I will be their God and they will be my children.

REVELATION 21:3–7

Prayer

Wielder of the cross, conquering hero, may my soul seek a kingdom away from the world's ways, making it more akin to the ways of heaven. May my soul seek your kingdom, and may it find rest there. Amen

Good Friday

Each year, when we read the story of the crucifixion of Christ, in whatever version, whether it is *The Dream of the Rood* or your favourite Bible version, we read it already knowing the end. We know the outcome of what is going on, but that doesn't make it any less emotionally connecting and spiritually powerful. Like watching films or television series which we have watched before, where we know what is going to happen in the end, we can still become engrossed in the thrilling and heart-wrenching scenes in the middle of the story. In that same way, despite the fact that for the past couple of days we have looked at the post-death scenes of *The Dream of the Rood*, I hope you find that as we look today at Christ on the cross, you will still be able to connect with this part of the story.

In this section of the story, *The Dream of the Rood* switches into a more traditional view. We get physical descriptions of what is happening and of Christ. Although it is still the Rood talking, we get descriptions of the nails being driven into them both, into the wood through the body of Christ; of blood flowing and drenching the wood. Despite the more physical perspective given in this scene, the Rood still becomes a part of the whole act. The Rood feels the insults of the people as they insult Christ; it describes how the nails opened gaping gashes in its own physical structure. The wood was intimately involved in the physical aspects of this act and was intricately aware of the spiritual significance of what was happening. This natural piece of creation understood. This is something which comes up in various parts of Celtic spirituality, both Christian and non-Christian – that the natural world has a relationship with, and is conscious of, its Creator, as suggested in Romans 8:9, 21. It is not only the Rood itself which has this connection, but all of creation.

The things which happened in the natural world during the time of the crucifixion are described not in a detached way, but in a way through which we might understand that creation was conscious and aware of what was happening. The earthquake and the darkness covering the sky are both expressed with a sense of awareness and consciousness and, finally, at the point of Christ dying, it says, 'All creation wept, wailed for the death of the King; Christ was on the cross.'[97] All creation is worded to mean all created things. The whole of the physical creation knew and could feel what was happening in that moment.

Although this section of *The Dream of the Rood* is quite short in comparison to the whole saga, it is, of course, the moment upon which all things hinge. The lead-up is simply building the story, as any good storyteller does, and the following sections, which we have already looked at, speak of the effect of the work of the cross for all things for all eternity.

The Dream of the Rood doesn't linger or labour the point of Christ dying, but neither does it pull any punches. The statement 'Christ was on the cross' is a profound and incredible statement. The Cosmic Christ, as described at the start of the gospel of John, which was well known to the Celtic Christians, was there, lifeless. Lifeless! The one through whom all life comes (John 1:3–4), who was life itself incarnate (1 John 1:1–2), was now life-*less*. This moment is worth a time to pause and reflect upon…

Contemplation

The Cosmic Christ, that is, the Christ who is from all eternity, who is the same yesterday, today and forever (Hebrews 13:8), who became incarnate and was restricted to the form of humanity, now nailed to the cross, lacks that which he gave to all things – life. Christ was on the cross. Pause and contemplate this.

Reading

As they went out, they came upon a man from Cyrene named Simon; they compelled this man to carry his cross. And when they came to a place called Golgotha (which means Place of a Skull), they offered him wine to drink, mixed with gall; but when he tasted it, he would not drink it. And when they had crucified him, they divided his clothes among themselves by casting lots; then they sat down there and kept watch over him. Over his head they put the charge against him, which read, 'This is Jesus, the King of the Jews.'

Then two bandits were crucified with him, one on his right and one on his left. Those who passed by derided him, shaking their heads and saying, 'You who would destroy the temple and build it in three days, save yourself! If you are the Son of God, come down from the cross.' In the same way the chief priests also, along with the scribes and elders, were mocking him, saying, 'He saved others; he cannot save himself. He is the King of Israel; let him come down from the cross now, and we will believe in him. He trusts in God; let God deliver him now, if he wants to; for he said, "I am God's Son."' The bandits who were crucified with him also taunted him in the same way.

From noon on, darkness came over the whole land until three in the afternoon. And about three o'clock Jesus cried with a loud voice, 'Eli, Eli, lema sabachthani?' that is, 'My God, my God, why have you forsaken me?' When some of the bystanders heard it, they said, 'This man is calling for Elijah.' At once one of them ran and got a sponge, filled it with sour wine, put it on a stick, and gave it to him to drink. But the others said, 'Wait, let us see whether Elijah will come to save him.' Then Jesus cried again with a loud voice and breathed his last. At that moment the curtain of the temple was torn in two, from top to bottom. The earth shook, and the rocks were split. The tombs also were opened, and many bodies of the saints who had fallen asleep were raised. After his resurrection they came out of the tombs and entered the holy city and appeared to many. Now when the centurion and those with him, who were keeping watch over Jesus, saw the earthquake and what took place, they were terrified and said, 'Truly this man was God's Son!'

Many women were also there, looking on from a distance; they had followed Jesus from Galilee and had provided for him.

MATTHEW 27:32–55

Prayer

Thank you.

Holy Saturday

This day is often a quiet 'nothing' day. We have been through the trauma of Good Friday yesterday, and we wait in anticipation for the celebration and resurrection of Easter Sunday tomorrow. But what do we do on the Saturday? What is there to think about? What do we focus on? Well, for us on our Lenten journey, we are going to absorb ourselves in the Celtic and Anglo-Saxon tradition of imaginative storytelling. For our focus today, we are going to look at an Irish text known as 'The Evernew Tongue', which dates from the late ninth or early tenth century. This text is a conversation between some Hebrew sages and the spirit of the apostle Philip on Easter eve (Holy Saturday) about creation and the resurrected re-creation while they sit at the top of Mount Zion after a meeting which had gone on for a year and four months (and you thought your church meetings were long)!

The reason that this piece is called 'The Evernew Tongue' is because of the legend that the apostle Philip had his tongue cut out nine times to stop him preaching, but each time a new tongue grew back so that he could continue to preach God's word. Therefore, he tells the sages, 'The people of heaven know me as the Evernew Tongue.'[98] The language in which the Evernew Tongue speaks to the sages is a heavenly language, one which we will all speak when in heaven, one which, he says, 'Even the creatures of the sea, beasts, four-footed animals, birds, serpents, and demons know.'[99] This resurrection language will be one with which we will all be able to commune with all living creatures. What a wonderful idea! Once again, we see here the Celtic belief that all of creation has a connection and relationship with the Creator. All the living things on the earth and in the heavenly realms know this language in which the Evernew Tongue speaks, and when we are resurrected we will know it too.

Although the text of this speaks about creation at the beginning of time, the Evernew Tongue tells the sages that this is also about the power of the resurrection of Christ, hence why it is told in the fading light of Easter eve. The Evernew Tongue says:

> All the world rose with [Christ], for the essence of all the elements was in the body that Jesus assumed.[100] For if the Lord had not suffered on behalf of the race of Adam, and risen from the dead, then Judgement Day would mean the destruction of the whole world and all the descendants of Adam. No creature of sea or land would be reborn… There would be neither land nor kindred, living or dead, in the world, only hell and heaven, if the Lord had not come back to redeem them. All would be destroyed without hope of restoration.[101]

The power of the resurrection is therefore contemplated here on the eve of the day of celebration. Tomorrow, the fast ends. Tomorrow, the sorrow abates. The grand celebration of the resurrection of Christ was a huge feast for the Celtic Christians. But for now, for Holy Saturday, Easter eve, just like the ancient Celtic Christians, before the festivities begin and the celebration feasts are laid out for Resurrection Day, we quietly contemplate the power of the resurrection of Christ, and what that means to us all, not just humans, but all of creation.

Contemplation

As we wait for the coming celebration, the coming life of the resurrection, pause and contemplate the power of that act, what that meant for the disciples at the time and what it has meant to every disciple since, including us today – but not only us, but for the whole creation.

Reading

I consider that the sufferings of this present time are not worth comparing with the glory about to be revealed to us. For the creation waits with eager longing for the revealing of the children of God; for the creation was subjected to futility, not of its own will but by the will of the one who subjected it, in hope that the creation itself will be set free from its bondage to decay and will obtain the freedom of the glory of the children of God. We know that the whole creation has been groaning in labour pains until now; and not only the creation, but we ourselves, who have the first fruits of the Spirit, groan inwardly while we wait for adoption, the redemption of our bodies. For in hope we were saved. Now hope that is seen is not hope. For who hopes for what is seen? But if we hope for what we do not see, we wait for it with patience.

ROMANS 8:18–25

Prayer

Christ who knew death, God who felt the loss of life, as we ready ourselves for resurrection, show me the power which this brings. I ask you, Lord, God of the universe, to release that resurrection power into my life today. Amen

Celebration
for **Easter Sunday**

Christ is risen!
He is risen indeed!
Alleluia!
Alleluia!

Let us celebrate and feast and rejoice as the
Celtic saints did at the end of the fast of Lent.
Let the new life of resurrection begin!

Notes

1 For a more detailed explanation, see the introduction to David Cole, *40 Days with the Celtic Saints* (BRF, 2017).

2 Oliver Davies, *Celtic Spirituality* (Paulist Press, 1999), p. 49.

3 Davies, *Celtic Spirituality*, p. 327.

4 Found in Davies, *Celtic Spirituality*, p. 369.

5 Davies, *Celtic Spirituality*, p. 369.

6 The original Irish word used is *glas* and this can be translated as either 'blue' or 'green'.

7 Davies, *Celtic Spirituality*, p. 370.

8 Kenneth McIntosh, *Water from an Ancient Well: Celtic spirituality for modern life* (Anamchara Books, 2011), p. 109.

9 McIntosh, *Water from an Ancient Well*, p. 110.

10 McIntosh, *Water from an Ancient Well*, p. 113.

11 Henry L. Carringan Jr, *The Wisdom of the Desert Fathers and Mothers* (Paraclete Press, 2010), p. xv.

12 Carringan Jr, *The Wisdom of the Desert Fathers and Mothers*, p. xvi.

13 Thomas Merton, *The Wisdom of the Desert* (New Directions, 1970), p. 10.

14 See **ria.ie/cathach-psalter-st-columba**.

15 A translation of this story can be found in Davies, *Celtic Spirituality*, from p. 155 onwards.

16 Prayer attributed to Columba of Iona.

17 Katherine Lack, *The Eagle and the Dove: The spirituality of the Celtic Saint Columbanus* (Triangle, 2000), p. 73.

18 Lack, *The Eagle and the Dove*, p. 73.

19 Esther De Waal, *Celtic Light: A tradition rediscovered* (Fount publishers, 1997), pp. 40, 42.

20 'Sermon eight', found in Davies, *Celtic Spirituality*, p. 355.

21 Merton, *The Wisdom of the Desert*, p. 6.

22 Ray Simpson, *Celtic Daily Light: A spiritual journey through the year* (Kevin Mayhew, 2003), October 13.

23 Uinseann Ó Maidín, *The Celtic Monk* (Cistercian Publications, 1996), p. 8.

24 Ó Maidín, *The Celtic Monk*, p. 7.
25 Thomas O'Loughlin, *Celtic Theology* (Continuum, 2005), p. 167.
26 For more information, visit **aidanandhilda.org.uk**.
27 Simon Reed, as well as being an Anglican Priest, is currently one of the Guardians of the Community of Aidan and Hilda.
28 Simon Reed, *Creating Community* (BRF, 2013).
29 Simon Reed, *Followers of the Way* (BRF, 2017), p. 26.
30 Reed, *Followers of the Way*, p. 28. For more on Simon's great insights on the biblical basis for a Rule of Life, read his essay in the appendix of Ray Simpson, *High Street Monasteries* (Kevin Mayhew, 2009).
31 Ray Simpson, as well as being a retired Anglican Priest, is the Founding Guardian of the Community of Aidan and Hilda.
32 Ray Simpson, *A Pilgrim Way: New Celtic Monasticism for everyday people* (Kevin Mayhew, 2005), pp. 7, 9.
33 Patrick Henry (ed.), *Benedict's Dharma: Buddhists reflect on the Rule of Saint Benedict* (Riverhead Books, 2001), p. 1.
34 Simpson, *A Pilgrim Way*, pp. 7–8.
35 Thomas O'Loughlin, *The Didache: A window on the earliest Christians* (Baker Academic, 2010), p. 23.
36 O'Loughlin, *The Didache*, pp. 23–24.
37 O'Loughlin, *The Didache*, pp. 30–31.
38 Maxwell Stamford (tr.), *Early Christian Writings* (Penguin Books, 1987), pp. 191–93.
39 The following is an edited and adapted version of the introduction to my book *Passing the Harp: Four Celtic allegories* (Anamchara Books, 2015).
40 David Adam, *The Cry of the Deer: Meditations on the hymn of St Patrick* (Triangle/SPCK, 2000), p. xiv.
41 Found in numerous hymn books.
42 C.F. Alexander's translation of St Patrick's Breastplate prayer – final two stanzas.
43 For a version of this sung in Irish Gaelic, see Máire Brennan's track on her album *Whisper to the wild water*.
44 Found in Gerald Murphy, *Early Irish Lyrics* (Oxford Books, 1956).
45 See Wednesday in Week 4 (p. 99).
46 From the versified version of 'Be thou my vision' by Eleanor Hull (1860–1935).
47 For more on Cædmon, see his entry in my book *40 Days with the Celtic Saints*.
48 Found in Robert Boenig (tr.), *Anglo-Saxon Spirituality: Selected writings* (Paulist Press, 2000), p. 168.

49 Davies, *Celtic Spirituality*, p. 43.
50 Fiona Bowie and Oliver Davies, *Celtic Christian Spirituality: An anthology of medieval and modern sources* (SPCK, 1997), p. 31.
51 Bowie and Davies, *Celtic Christian Spirituality*, p. 32.
52 A biblical term for the devil. See John 12:30–32 (NIV) for example.
53 Bowie and Davies, *Celtic Christian Spirituality*, p. 45.
54 Bowie and Davies, *Celtic Christian Spirituality*, p. 45.
55 Italics mine.
56 The band IONA have a wonderful version of 'When I survey the wondrous cross', for example.
57 J. Philip Newell, *Listening to the Heartbeat of God: A Celtic spirituality* (Paulist Press, 1997), p. 15.
58 B.R. Rees, *Pelagius: Life and letters*, vol. 2 (The Boydell Press, 2004), pp. 44–45.
59 Rodney Newman, *Journeys with Celtic Christians* (Abingdon Press, 2015), p. 55.
60 Newell, *Listening to the Heartbeat of God*, p. 15.
61 John Scotus Eriugena, *Periphyseon: On the division of nature* (Wipf & Stock, 2011), pp. 282–23.
62 A printable translation can be found here: **faithandworship.com/pdf/stowe%20missal.pdf**.
63 O'Loughlin, *Celtic Theology*, pp. 128–29.
64 Both these Triads can be found in Judith Millidge, *The Celtic Day Book* (Thorsons, 1998), pp. 10, 41.
65 Davies, *Celtic Spirituality*, pp. 311–12.
66 Davies, *Celtic Spirituality*, p. 312.
67 See my book *The Mystic Path of Meditation: Beginning a Christ-centred journey* (Anamchara Books, 2013).
68 Davies, *Celtic Spirituality*, p. 312.
69 See **faithandworship.com/pdf/stowe%20missal.pdf**, p. 40.
70 Picture taken from **faithandworship.com/pdf/stowe%20missal.pdf**, p. 40.
71 Davies, *Celtic Spirituality*, p. 313.
72 Lyrics from the song 'Broken Saviour' by Anam Caras Band. Used with permission. Copyright © Terry Braithwaite and Jackie Mills.
73 For a fuller description see O'Loughlin, *Celtic Theology*, pp. 135–36.
74 Davies, *Celtic Spirituality*, p. 312.
75 The Rule of Columbanus, 'Monks rules: of a monk's perfection, rule 4'. Found at **celt.ucc.ie/published/T201052/index.html**.
76 O'Loughlin, *Celtic Theology*, pp. 128–29.

77 This chant can be found in Davies, *Celtic Spirituality*, pp. 314–16.

78 Davies, *Celtic Spirituality*, p. 315.

79 McIntosh, *Water from an Ancient Well*, p. 71.

80 The *Carmina Gadelica* (the 'Song of the Gauls/Celts') is a collection of oral tradition prayers collated at the turn of the 19th to 20th century by Alexander Carmichael in the highlands of Scotland. As these prayers and poems were all oral tradition, none of them can be guaranteed to be older than two or three generations from when they were collected. However, they reflect so well and so similarly what we do know of the ancient historic Celtic peoples and their spirituality, the verses from the *Carmina Gadelica* are commonly interwoven with the ancient thought, prayers and teaching of the Celtic Christians.

81 Alexander Carmichael, *Carmina Gadelica* (Floris Books, 2006), p. 278.

82 A printable English translation can be found here: **yorku.ca/inpar/Dream_Rood_Kennedy.pdf** or a version in its original Old English language can be found in Bruce Dickins and Alan S.C. Cross (eds), *The Dream of the Rood* (Methuen's Old English Library, 1964).

83 Boenig, *Anglo-Saxon Spirituality*, p. 42.

84 Reflects the opening line of *The Dream of the Rood*.

85 Boenig, *Anglo-Saxon Spirituality*, p. 260.

86 Kevin Crossley-Holland (trans), *The Anglo-Saxon World: An anthology* (Oxford University Press, 2009), p. 201.

87 Boenig, *Anglo-Saxon Spirituality*, p. 260.

88 Boenig, *Anglo-Saxon Spirituality*, p. 261.

89 Crossley-Holland, *The Anglo-Saxon World*, p. 202.

90 Boenig, *Anglo-Saxon Spirituality*, p. 261.

91 Crossley-Holland, *The Anglo-Saxon World*, p. 202.

92 Boenig, *Anglo-Saxon Spirituality*, p. 262.

93 Boenig, *Anglo-Saxon Spirituality*, p. 262.

94 Boenig, *Anglo-Saxon Spirituality*, p. 262.

95 Crossley-Holland, *The Anglo-Saxon World*, p. 204.

96 Crossley-Holland, *The Anglo-Saxon World*, p. 204.

97 Crossley-Holland, *The Anglo-Saxon World*, p. 201.

98 Boenig, *Anglo-Saxon Spirituality*, p. 323.

99 Boenig, *Anglo-Saxon Spirituality*, p. 323.

100 Remember back to Ash Wednesday and the collection of elements in the creation of Adam.

101 Boenig, *Anglo-Saxon Spirituality*, pp. 323–24.

This inspirational book takes the reader through Advent to the celebration of Christmas through the eyes and beliefs of Celtic Christianity. Starting in November and reflecting on Jesus' coming at his birth as well as into our lives by the Holy Spirit and at the world's end, the author offers a unique approach to the season to help you gain a new sense of wonder in the birth of Jesus, the Saviour of the world.

Celtic Advent
40 days of devotions to Christmas
David Cole
978 0 85746 744 7 £8.99

brfonline.org.uk